TEXT - ENGLISH 120 - 1974
ENGLISH 121

D1637255

*English Through
Poetry Writing*

English Through Poetry Writing

A Creative Approach for Schools

BRIAN POWELL
M.A.(McGill), Dip.Ed.(Oxford), D.P.A.(London)

HEINEMANN
LONDON

Heinemann Educational Books Ltd

LONDON EDINBURGH MELBOURNE TORONTO
SINGAPORE JOHANNESBURG AUCKLAND
IBADAN HONG KONG NAIROBI
NEW DELHI

© Brian Powell 1968

ISBN 0 435 14700 5

First published in Australia by Ian Novak
Publishing Co., Sydney as Volume IV in the
Teaching Methods Series edited by
Professor W. F. Connell, Professor of Education,
University of Sydney, and
Professor W. H. Frederick, Emeritus Professor of Education,
University of Melbourne

First published in Great Britain 1968
Reprinted 1970

Published by
Heinemann Educational Books Ltd
48 Charles Street, London W1X 8AH
Printed in Great Britain by
Morrison & Gibb Ltd, London and Edinburgh

CONTENTS

PART II—ADVANCED

ACKNOWLEDGMENTS

I want to thank those who have given particular advice and encouragement in the shaping of this book:

Alice Baldwin, McGill University, Montreal; Mark Bishop, Cranbrook School, Sydney; Lester Bullen, Collins' School, Yukon; Mike Charlesworth, Repton, England; John Clark, The Dragon School, Oxford; Professor W. F. Connell, University of Sydney; Dr J. R. Darling, former Headmaster, Geelong Grammar School; Emeritus Professor W. H. Frederick, University of Melbourne; Dr John Harley, McGill University, Montreal; Dr Harold Loukes, Oxford University; George Lowe, The Grange School, Santiago, Chile; David Mallick, Normanhurst High School, Sydney; Paul McKeown, Canberra Grammar School, Canberra; Olma Mignacca, Avalon Beach School, Sydney; Harry Nicolson, Cranbrook School, Sydney; Dr Steven Penton, Lower Canada College, Montreal; Bill Perkins, University of Tasmania; and my parents and the rest of my family for their ever-present support.

I am also grateful to numerous other colleagues and friends who have helped me and made me welcome when I visited their schools.

This book would never have become a reality, however, without the enthusiasm of many young writers. To them, I owe most of all.

Brian Powell,
38 Church Hill,
Montreal 6, Canada.

PREFACE

OSTENSIBLY about poetry, the reach of this book is much wider. The improvement in command of language through the understanding of meaning, the cultivation of expressiveness, the refining of ideas and the selection and arrangement of words to fit them are among the principal concerns of all English teachers. These are the matters with which this book deals.

The programme suggested here is based on practical experience. Every poem in the book has been collected by the author from classes he has taught in Canada, U.S.A., England, Australia, U.S.S.R., and Chile. But the work is not merely a report of the efforts of one inspired teacher. The methods advocated have been widely tried and proved. Each poem reproduced here can be matched by other poems produced by other pupils taught by experienced teachers or teachers in training who have been stirred by the author's work and have successfully adopted his ideas and practices.

In presenting his material the author goes direct into the classroom, explaining from the beginning of the book how to deal with elementary and, subsequently, more advanced poetry-writing. He summarises his basic ideas and procedures in a final chapter dealing with the fundamental principles that can be seen emerging from the programme as the reader works his way through it.

Teachers of English will find Mr. Powell's ideas stimulating, and productive of much hard-work and enjoyment among pupils.

W. F. CONNELL
University of Sydney
W. H. FREDERICK
University of Melbourne

FOREWORD

It is an axiom of modern approaches to the teaching of English that the less the teacher does, and the more the student does, the better it is. In the words of the Chinese proverb, "I hear and I forget; I see and I remember; I do and I understand." But most teachers know the problem of getting boys and girls to "do". We cannot simply say to them, "Write", because they cannot do it. We cannot "tell" them about it, because the secret of creation is not to be talked about.

This book offers a carefully articulated method whereby any teacher can offer the thrust to action, the spark to creation. At its heart, the method is essentially simple, for it is no more than a meeting of elemental forms with elemental experiences: it offers the narrowest possible gap for the spark to leap. Students who thus quail before the problems of sustained writing at length are stirred to action by the specificity of the situation in which they are placed, and find themselves succeeding through sheer concentration. And from this initial success, the method progresses to greater complexity and sophistication. It is a method that has been developed to its present simplicity through years of experiment and argument and criticism; and what remains has the validity, as near as may be in the world of creative imagination, of a laboratory process, repeatable wherever the conditions are right.

Brian Powell is a teacher of genius, with a rare insight into the practical situation and an untiring zest for enquiry into the reason why. As a student in the Oxford Department of Education he won one of our rare Distinctions in the Theory and Practice of Education; and since then he has explored this field of creative writing to the point where any teacher can take the tools in his hand and begin to set the sparks flying for himself.

Harold Loukes
Reader in Education, University of Oxford

"O! For a Muse of fire that would ascend
The brightest heaven of invention."

(Shakespeare)

"Oh then, if in my lagging lines you miss
The roll, the rise, the carol, the creation."

(Hopkins)

"The spider's touch how exquisitely fine
Feels at each thread and lives along the line."

(Pope)

CHAPTER *1*

INTRODUCTION

ON TREMBLING WINGS

An introduction by three young writers:

THE SWAN

White bird on light wings,
Soundless through the clear blue sky,
Gentle, god-like swan.

(K.M., Geelong Grammar School, Australia.)

THE FOAL

Delicate small one,
With wobbly legs trying hard,
The foal is standing.

(M.B., Winchester College, England.)

AUTUMN

Geese are flying in a wedge,
Southward from the Arctic edge;
Nobles in a barren sky
Honking omens as they fly.

(R.G., Lower Canada College, Montreal, Canada.)

This book is about the writing of poetry. It is designed for teachers, and presents a programme which requires pupils to write poetry themselves. In this way they are led to a fuller understanding of language by actual experience in writing. They learn through doing. The attempt to express themselves through poetry should help pupils to gain an insight into the skills that every writer must develop: a way of looking at things accurately; a way of experiencing things acutely; and a way of expressing things lucidly.

The programme of work outlined in this book strives to encourage pupils in a systematic way to follow up their experiences with expression, and not to be satisfied until they have transmitted their feelings with accuracy.

As a teacher, I have tried to develop a programme that will help young writers to become aware of their experiences, and later write about them with sincerity. The creative act forces pupils to make sense of jumbled life experiences, and to bring into focus thoughts which may, at first, be unorganized. The teacher should be able to help his pupils by narrowing the direction of their attention.

Ideas are crystallizations of what is already present in the mind from experience. The process of writing is a bringing to the surface of feelings which, but for the creative act, might never have been expressed at all. Hence poetry writing gives the pupil an opportunity to transform his feelings into productive force. Through it, he is learning to make decisions. Each line he writes may be tested to see if it belongs. His selection is a matter of choice. He is immediately faced with the result of this choice, and here his critical capacities are brought into play. He is thus learning to solve problems, and this requires a degree of self-discipline. It is mainly this self-discipline which enables the pupil to travel the road from the creative impulse to the finished work.

I have said that writing effectively is a discipline demanding hard work. This work can be rewarding, however, when the pupil feels that he is writing with a purpose. The programme outlined in these pages is the result of ten years of work in schools in a number of countries. I have rejected any approaches which were of little help to pupils. The stages that remain have been tested in numerous situations with the help and advice of teachers, to whom I am most grateful.

HOW IS THE PROGRAMME CONSTRUCTED?

The programme itself is made up of three interdependent elements basic to good writing: form, content, and evaluation. I have constructed these elements as follows:

The *form* series gives the pupil a number of structures for the shaping of his writing.

The *content* categories present him with suggestions for subject matter.

The *evaluation* exercises are designed to help him improve his expression.

The individual classroom period is the central unit of the programme, and almost all writing takes place within it. Each period should contain a brief introduction by the teacher, time for writing, and an opportunity at the end for pupils to read their work.

I have presented the elements of form, content, and evaluation in this order because experiment has convinced me that this is the order in which they are of most help. The greatest need of the beginner is for guidance, not with what to say, but with how to say it. For this reason I introduce the form stages first, since they seem to provide pupils with the means whereby they can most readily release their ideas. I lead young writers through a series of structural devices, starting with ones that are rigid in form, and then moving with each stage toward greater freedom as the pupils gain experience. After they have been working successfully for some time on subjects of their own choice, I introduce the content categories which give them suggestions for material. When they reach the stage of wanting to improve their technique, I bring in evaluation exercises to provide for this need.

I hope that this programme will achieve two goals: that it will help pupils to write with more accuracy and effectiveness; and that it will help them to derive enjoyment and a sense of accomplishment from doing so. I also hope that teachers will get satisfaction from attempting to teach English expression through this poetry writing approach.

HOW IS POETRY DEFINED FOR THE PURPOSES OF THIS WRITING
PROGRAMME?

In order to arrive at a working definition of the term "poetry" for the purposes of this programme, the teacher may have to

attack some misconceptions that may exist in the minds of beginners. The pupils should realize that poetry need not necessarily
be metrical, nor need it have any rigid pattern or rhyme scheme.
It certainly should not merely conform to the definition given by
a pupil that "Poetry is something that rhymes nice and learns
easy." It must not be devoted exclusively to elevated themes, or
to subjects which some may regard as poetic such as clouds,
daffodils or immortality.

Young writers should be encouraged to realize that poetry is a
form of expression more concise than prose, usually characterized
by concrete imagery. If it is to be sincere, poetry should deal with
subjects that genuinely interest young people, whether these be
racing cars, surfing, sewing, or the Tijuana Brass. Once the pupils
realize this, they should have less uncertainty in choosing their
topics than if they had a narrow understanding of what poetry is.

I have found the following four definitions helpful in attempting to broaden the ideas pupils have of what constitutes poetry:

"Poetry is the language of the imagination and the passions."

(William Hazlitt)

"Poetry is the synthesis of hyacinths and biscuits."

(Carl Sandburg)

"Poetry is the record of the best and happiest moments of the
best and happiest minds."

(Percy Bysshe Shelley)

"Poetry is, among other things, a kind of hypnosis; it puts one
part of us asleep in order that another part may become
more aware, more receptive, more active."

(C. Day Lewis)

The fourth definition brings out an important point. Poetry
should not be primarily concerned with straight reasoning or
logic; they are that "part" which is "put asleep". Nobody wears
all his thoughts and emotions on his sleeve. They lie to some
degree hidden. Every man has dreams, longings, and fears regardless of how much he may try to disguise them. It is from these
depths that poetry should speak.

Let me, with the help of two young pupils, propose one further definition: poetry is an attempt by a writer to capture in words a moment that, for him, is meaningful. The poet is seeking to do much the same thing with his pen as is the artist with his brush, or the photographer with his shutter, when they try to capture on canvas or film some fleeting expression or action.

One boy has put it this way:

> Poetry is a brief vision of ecstasy,
> Gone—
> But caught forever.
>
> (R.M., Canberra Grammar School, Australia.)

A second pupil felt poised between past and present when he wrote:

> Frozen, as in ice, years past
> That moment lingers still—
> Silent, yet alive,
> The moment lives for evermore.
>
> (G.H., Cranbrook School, Sydney, Australia.)

WHAT REWARDS DOES THE PROGRAMME OFFER THE PUPIL?

I have already outlined the opportunities that the programme offers to the pupil who wants to improve his command of language. It should offer him other benefits as well, however. Contact with living poetry should provide a humanizing influence in his daily routine, for poetry appeals to his aesthetic nature, to the sense of wonder in him. This sense of wonder is often dimmed by formalized instruction. He must be given opportunities to enjoy discovery, to release his enthusiasm, and even occasionally to be overwhelmed by things around him. What better way to do this than by attempting to express himself through poetry?

Imagine the situation as I took a class of thirteen-year-old boys outside on a late autumn afternoon in Canberra. The boys were excited as we walked through the leaves and attentive as we looked at the shape of a stark poplar. I asked them to go away for fifteen minutes, not to talk to each other, but to open wide their eyes and ears and write about anything they experienced. They moved to different places: one boy sat cross-legged beneath a spider-web as the sun turned it to gold; another lay on his back and looked skyward at the leaves falling around him; still another watched the wisps of thistledown that drifted through the air. All were silent as they wrote.

I called them back and we sat on the grass and listened to their haikus:[1]

POPLARS

Poplars tall and bare,
Surrendering to winter,
As they wait for spring.

(C.N., Canberra Grammar School, Australia.)

THISTLEDOWN

Floating through the air,
Quietly as a snowflake,
See the fuzzies run.

(A.H., Canberra Grammar School, Australia.)

THE TAP

Grey tap on the ground
Sitting in a clump of grass
Ugly little thing.

(P.D., Canberra Grammar School, Australia.)

Each boy had experienced a moment for himself, and made an attempt at conveying it which revealed promise, and which gave him pleasure at the same time.

To get to the finished product, however, much effort is needed. If the poem is to come at all, it must be preceded by the concentration required to pick the right word for the context, and the right combination of words to produce the desired effect. Here

---

[1] For a description of the haiku see Chapter 2.

lies the core of the writer's task without which nothing is accomplished.

On a recent visit to a school I was discussing word usage with a senior class and asked them: "What verb would you choose if you wanted to describe what the moon does at night?" One pupil suggested the word "glow", and most of his classmates nodded approval. Someone near the back of the room, however, raised his hand and said, "I don't think glow is the right word because, to me, it suggests warmth and heat. I might talk of a coal or an ember glowing—I can almost see a red or orange colour—but not the moon. There is no warmth connected with the moon. It sheds a cold light." He concluded his statement by offering the verb "gleam" as an alternative. This boy was starting to come to grips with the realities of effective writing, and to understand some of its demands.

IS THIS POETRY WRITING PROGRAMME ONLY FOR THE ADVANCED?

The reader may ask whether the programme is suitable for pupils of all ability levels, or whether it is only for the advanced. My experience has been that the programme can be of as much benefit to the mediocre pupil and the slow learner as to the more gifted. It offers the less able pupil an outlet for self-expression which he needs but is seldom able to enjoy in school. Achievement in creative work need have no direct relationship with native intelligence. Slower pupils see and feel like others, and they may write of their experiences as directly as faster pupils. In fact, if I had to generalize—and generalizations are dangerous—I would say that over the years I have got just as much work of quality from pupils who stand below the half-way mark in their classes as from those who stand above it. Certainly this division would hold true over the full range of examples in this book. The work of less academically able pupils often has a genuineness that is sometimes lacking in the attempts of those who are more academically gifted.

The teacher has a responsibility, however, to all the pupils in his classes, and they should all be able to derive benefit from attempting to express themselves through poetry. Pupils often become actively involved in playing instruments in their music periods, or in painting pictures in their art periods. Likewise they should have an opportunity to write poems during some of their English periods.

CHART OF THE PROGRAMME

PART I—INTRODUCTORY

FORM STAGES (as in Chapter 2)	CONTENT CATEGORIES (as in Chapter 3)	EVALUATION EXERCISES (as in Chapter 4)
INTRODUCTORY EXERCISES	SOURCES OF INSPIRATION	INITIAL CRITERIA OF JUDGMENT
Reading	Activities	
Rhythm	Surroundings	
Observation	Reflections	
Sensory awareness		
Diction		CONSTRUCTIVE CRITICISM
Imagery		
Imagination		
	SENSORY STIMULI	
	Sight	
DYLAN THOMAS PORTRAITS	Sound	PERSONAL ASSESSMENT
Sight	Feeling	
Sound	Smell	
	Taste	
EZRA POUND COUPLETS		
		A FRAMEWORK FOR EVALUATION
THE FORM POEM		Content
	THEMES FROM THE ARTS	Technique
THE SYLLABLE POEM	Literature	Impact
HAIKU	Art	
	Movement	
COMPOSITE SEQUENCE		
REVIEW SERIES		

PART II—ADVANCED

FORM STAGES
(as in Chapter 5)

COMPLETED IMAGE VARIATIONS
- Chinese introduction
- Precise skeleton
- Contrast
- Free range

FORMAL PATTERNS
- Rhymed couplets
- Quatrain
- Ballad
- Parody
- Sonnet
- Further forms

PRIME-THE-PUMP INTRODUCTIONS
- The group poem
- Individual framework
- Imaginative first lines

OPTIC PATTERNS

EXPERIMENTAL STRUCTURES
- Formless poems
- Audio poems
- Inside-out poems

FORM FRAMEWORK

COMPOSITE SEQUENCE

CONTENT CATEGORIES
(as in Chapter 6)

THEMES FROM THE ARTS
- Sculpture
- Music
- Drama

DIRECT EXPERIENCES
- Research into the topic
- Situation outline
- Visits to places of interest

TRIGGERS

EVALUATION EXERCISES
(as in Chapter 7)

ASSESSMENT OF POETRY
- Techniques of Understanding
- Comparison of Poems

THE CRAFTSMANSHIP OF THE POET

OUTSIDE-CLASS PROJECTS

It remains for the teacher to encourage within the classroom the type of atmosphere that will enable creative effort to grow. He must destroy any suggestion that poetry writing is only for the soft, the intellectual, or the eccentric. He should show his pupils that it demands a perception, a fibre, and a certain toughness of spirit, as well as a tenderness. Writing poetry is another way of trying to live the full life in which all can share.

A CHART OF THE PROGRAMME

On the two preceding pages there is a chart for the guidance of teachers about to begin. It should be regarded as an outline only, and not as an inflexible framework. I never adopt exactly the same approach or sequence of stages with any two classes because no two groups are exactly alike. If the programme is to work, it must be applied by each teacher as *his* programme for his own particular class, and not as mine.

The programme is based on a number of principles with which every teacher should be familiar. These are brought together in Chapter Eight. I suggest, however, that the teacher should know these principles before he faces his first class and perhaps makes errors in presentation of which he may be unaware at the time, but which he may find difficult to rectify later.

The stages presented in the chart correspond to those outlined in the book. For convenience of usage they appear in two parts, introductory and advanced.

GO WITH WINGS

The effective teacher should act as a human bridge between childhood and adulthood. If he is to help his pupils leap the gap between these worlds—and surely this is what education is about—he must try to maintain communication with both himself.

Poetry should serve him well in this respect. At its best, poetry links the romance of childhood with the realism of adulthood; it blends the enthusiasm of youth with the perception of older age. The pupil who writes poetry is developing these links.

Part I

INTRODUCTORY

CHAPTER 2

FORM STAGES

INTRODUCTORY EXERCISES

This first section presents exercises in seven categories: reading, rhythm, observation, sensory awareness, diction, imagery, and imagination. The beginner should do these exercises as a preparation for subsequent stages of the writing programme.

READING: Every teacher should compile an anthology of poems for use in poetry reading and speaking. These should be selected for their subject appeal and rhythm, and illustrate the fact that poetry is written to be read aloud. The teacher should provide training in the skills of oral work such as tempo and expression. He should do some reading himself, and get the class to imitate the different speeds and inflections that he has demonstrated. For instance, he should show the pupils that a line describing the movement of an express train should be read with urgency and a quick tempo, not slowly as one might read a line describing a swan flying at sunset. He should attempt, through his expression, to portray the character of his subject.

The following piece should be suitable for group speaking as it contains simple repetitive lines which are said each time with increased intensity:

SURFING

Surfing in the morning,
Surfing through the day,
Let the waves roll higher,
Let the waves roll higher,
Let the waves roll higher,
Sweep us far away!

Further exercises on poetry reading should include verse speaking in unison (using pieces such as "The Wendigo", by Ogden Nash); dialogue and two-part work ("The Circus", by C. J. Dennis); mime ("The Three Witches", from Macbeth); individual interpretations ("Carnival of Animals", by Kenneth Slessor), or plays for voices (excerpts from "Under Milk Wood", by Dylan Thomas).

RHYTHM: A characteristic of poetry is that it usually has some basic rhythm. This is not to be confused with rhyme—an element often considered by the beginner as a restriction which produces the "school-fool-stool-rule" type of poem, or which forces him into writing which may be insincere. Rhyme may prove a shackle. Rhythm should be a natural, positive force.

The teacher should suggest a number of exercises as a means of helping pupils to develop their sense of rhythm.

1. Language must suit the theme or mood. The pupils may be asked to give some examples of:

> Quiet words
> Noisy words
> Slow words
> Quick words

What letters and sounds are characteristic of each?
In what type of situation would you use each?

What would have been the effect if you had used another word instead?

2. Compile a list of words each of which has two beats, an unaccented one, followed by an accented one, e.g.:

> ā | wáy, tō | dáy, ūn | séen

Tap or clap in time to the beat they suggest.

3. Complete these sentences using mostly short sounds:
> Into the shop . . . .
> Up jumped the dog as . . . .

Complete these using long sounds:
> The moon rose . . . .
> The eagle glided . . . .

4. Write a line to suggest:
   An express train
   A horseman riding
   A child asleep
   Wind in the trees
   A greyhound running.

Move your hands, arms, and shoulders in time to the line you
have written.

5. Make some of the noises heard in the traffic. Write on the
blackboard some of the sounds you have made. Produce the
sounds all together. Do the same for:

| machinery | rocket launching |
| animals | war. |

OBSERVATION: With little formal introduction, the teacher should
display three or four large pictures to the class each featuring
colour, movement, or some other distinctive characteristic. After
giving a few moments for observation, he should cover up the
pictures and ask a series of questions, requiring either oral or
one-word written answers.

The results should demonstrate that most pupils do not observe
accurately without some specific prior training. In order to
emphasize this point, the teacher might show the pictures again,
focusing on the details which most failed to notice the first time.

This idea can be extended by asking each pupil the colour of
his own socks, the licence number of his father's car, the nature
of the pictures on the walls of his classroom, or any other seemingly obvious details.

In a further extension of this exercise, the teacher should display
a number of thought-provoking pictures and ask the pupils to
concentrate on some specific element such as sense, action, feeling,
or idea. The young writers should attempt to capture the essence
of the picture by giving it a title in the form of a single word,
phrase, or complete sentence.

The appropriateness of various titles should be tested by discussion of such questions as the following:

1. Is the title clear and accurate?
2. Does it enable the viewer to see in a different light?
3. Has it given him new understanding?

By attempting to capture the spirit of a picture in words, the pupil is receiving training in a skill basic to poetry writing.

SENSORY AWARENESS: The appreciation of beauty is closely linked with an awareness through the senses. Much as a blind person develops his powers of hearing and touch, so should the pupil be encouraged to heighten his sensory awareness through various exercises. He should be asked to close his eyes while a number of stimuli are presented, either to the whole class at once, as with sound and smell, or to individuals one at a time, as with touch and taste. He should then be asked to:

1. Identify the stimulus in a single word.
2. Describe it as accurately as he can in a single sentence without naming it or giving obvious clues as to its identity.

If every pupil in a class has been exposed to a different stimulus, individual answers should be read out and guesses made as to what each pupil has tried to describe. If, on the other hand, the same stimulus has been used for everyone, a group verdict should be reached as to the most effective description. The teacher might arrange his stimuli according to senses, using some of the following suggestions:

1. *Sound*: rain, bird cries (or other recorded sounds), sharpening a pencil, tearing paper.
2. *Smell*: perfume, coffee, pepper, sawdust, newly-baked bread, wood smoke, cut grass.
3. *Touch*: velvet, silk, plasticine, sponge, soap, pine cone, or the face of any member of the class.
4. *Taste*: licorice, cheese, fruit-flavoured gum drops, salt.

An aim of these exercises is to make the pupil conscious of senses and of elements previously unconsidered.

DICTION: The following exercises are an extension of those above. They demonstrate that picking the exact word for any given context is an art demanding care. The teacher should emphasize in his introduction that a difference of detail between poetry and prose lies in the greater weight of meaning carried by the individual word in poetry. Statements such as the following might help to illustrate:

"The difference between the right word, and almost the right word, is like the difference between lightning and lightning bug."

(Edgar Allan Poe)

"The business of words in prose is primarily to state; in poetry not only to state but also, and sometimes primarily, to suggest."

(Livingston Lowes)

"The meaning of a word is not a set, cut-off thing like the move of a knight or pawn on a chessboard. It comes up with roots, with associations."

(Ezra Pound)

The importance of certain standards should be emphasized: originality, simplicity and restraint. The element of restraint is one that tends to be overlooked by those working with young writers, and hence it should command special attention. Too often the beginner thinks that exaggeration is a mark of good writing. He should be encouraged, if anything, to understate.

I frequently give pupils a word exercise which asks them, for example, to write down, within five seconds, the verb they would use to describe the sound of the wind rushing through the trees on a stormy night. After they have made their pressured response I tell them to reconsider their choice, taking up to five minutes to put down the word they feel is the most appropriate for the situation. They must not change their original word unless they feel they have a more accurate one. I have found that up to three-quarters of the pupils do change their original word. This indicates that the selection of the exact word is a demanding task, and that the pupil does well to examine the first word that jumps into his head. It may not be the best one he can produce if he really concentrates on it.

1. Make a list of words as follows:

    Words that describe pleasing smells.

        ,,   ,,   ,,   harsh sounds.

        ,,   ,,   ,,   sharp edges.

        ,,   ,,   ,,   shiny objects.

2. Make a list of "sound" words, arranged in order of intensity, dealing with:
   Explosives (begin with "pop").
   Animal noises (begin with "squeak").
   Traffic (begin with "hum").

3. Underline the word which expresses the meaning most precisely:
   The old brick building had (vanished, gone, departed, withdrawn) before the wreckers in a cloud of broken brick and plaster.
   The glow of their forges (shone, could be seen, was seen, blinked red) in the twilight.

4. Compose *specific* vivid phrases to replace the following *general*, colourless phrases:
   An expensive automobile.
   A dark night.
   A terrifying sight with an alarming sound.
   A sickening taste with an unpleasant smell.

5. The following statement uses the verbs "said" and "left" in a general sense:
   "No," he *said*, and *left* the room.
   Compose a number of specific variations of it, e.g.:
   "No," he moaned, and crept from the room.
   "No," he shrieked, and dashed from the room.
   "No," he sobbed, and stumbled from the room.
   "No," he lisped, and sidled from the room.
   "No," he whispered, and tiptoed from the room.
   Or: Create as many original synonyms as possible for such overworked words as beautiful, nice, happy, or good.

6. Describe the following as precisely as you can. Have a specific situation in mind, and use single words, or a single sentence at most:
   The sound of a typewriter.
   The feel of a dog's nose.
   The smell of an old attic.
   The taste of vinegar.
   The sensation in your stomach as you come down in an elevator.

These exercises should encourage the pupil to be more sensitive to the power of the exact word. As the painter must choose his colours with discrimination, so the young writer must exercise care in the selection of his words.

IMAGERY: The teacher should give a brief definition of imagery, emphasizing that it consists in creating resemblances and is characterized by the simile and metaphor. An image in poetry is a mental picture of an idea presented through sensory appeals which help the reader to evaluate the unknown in the light of the known. Since poetry communicates more by suggestion than by direct statement, images help the poet to make understandably concrete ideas that might otherwise remain abstract.

Some examples of figurative language should be given, such as:

(a) A cat wove itself in and out of the railings ....

(b) The yellow smoke that rubs its muzzle on the window panes,
Licks its tongue into the corners of the evening.

(c) The velvet hum of bees ....

  1. Complete the following:[1]
       The flags flapped like ....
       With sharp blue eyes like ....
       Like streamers long and gay ....
       Like a gleam of gold ....
       As bitter as ....

  2. Evaluate the following image using as your criteria the elements of:
       appropriateness
       conciseness
       originality
     The leaves were lipsticked with autumn.

     [The pupils should be trained to realize that this metaphor is weak because of the cacophonous effect produced by the word "lipsticked", as well as the artificial connotation it suggests, quite out of harmony with the subject, Nature.]

[1] At a later stage, any of these introductions might be extended into a poem.

3. Using images wherever possible, discuss:
   The colour blue.
   The feel of mud between your toes.
   The movement of a running kangaroo.
   The sound of a saw cutting down a tree.
   The taste of fruit ice-cream.
   The sight of moonlight on water.

IMAGINATION: Looking at the colours on an oily puddle is observation, but seeing pictures in them is imagination. For the poet, what is important is not so much the picture-taking power of his mind, but rather that picture-making power which enables him to capture significance unrecognized by the casual observer. Imagination is that power which helps the viewer to endow something quite ordinary with distinctive quality.

Exercises in this section illustrate the point that the pupil may develop his imagination by increasing his powers of perception; and by concentrating on the specific rather than on the general.

1. Answer the following questions:
   What does a lion look like?
   What does it think about?
   What would it say if it could talk?
   What does it make you think about?

2. Divide a page of your exercise book into two sections, one headed "description" and the other headed "imagery". Complete the sections in the following manner:

Subject	Description	Imagery
Jet sound	The jet makes a thunderous noise.	The jet engine roars like a rocket leaving the launching pad.
Soap bubble	The soap bubble is round, and contains various colours.	The soap bubble looks like a technicolor plastic sausage.

The following suggestions, representing each of the senses, might serve as useful topics for this approach:

Sight: snowflakes, cypress tree, candle flame, stars at night.
Sound: fire alarm, organ music, steam engine, surf.
Feeling: sandpaper, driving rapidly with the windshield
          open, cat's fur, fire.
Taste: onion, maple syrup.
Smell: sweet peas, eggs and bacon frying, seaweed.

The pupil should now be ready to proceed to the more formal stages of the poetry writing itself. The remainder of this chapter is devoted to the five forms which he is to undertake: the Dylan Thomas portrait, Ezra Pound couplet, form poem, syllable poem, and haiku. There is a concluding review sequence.

DYLAN THOMAS PORTRAITS

Concise couplet-type devices, based on the writing of Dylan Thomas,[2] are presented to promote an adventurous approach to the use of words, and in this sense are a sequel to the introductory exercises. They are designed to reduce stereotypes in the mind of the pupil as to how words should be employed, and to suggest original uses. Each portrait represents an attempt to capture the essence of its subject, and might be of two types: description or sound.

DESCRIPTION: The pupil should be given several models, each of which offers no rigid total pattern, but invariably begins in the same way: Did you ever see a ———?

  e.g.: Did you ever see an otter?
        Silvery-sided, fish-fanged, fierce-faced, mottled.

Portraits attempted by pupils should follow this pattern and should contain hyphenated words, double-barrelled expressions, nouns used as adjectives, and any other distinctive features that the young writer may devise. The teacher, in presenting the above illustration, should point out the original nature of the image "fish-fanged", perhaps even getting one of the pupils to illustrate it on the blackboard for added impact.

An effective portrait should contain either three, four or five parts; less than three will be too few to establish anything distinc-

[2] I have developed this device as a result of interest in the way Dylan Thomas uses words, particularly in a work like *Under Milk Wood*.

tive, while the portrait will probably grow cumbersome with more than five parts. Animals, objects or people should present suitable subjects for these portraits:

> Did you ever see a snake?
> Zig-zagging, fork-tongued, elastic-jawed.
>> (B.L., The Grange School, Santiago, Chile.)

> Did you ever see a school boy?
> Shirt-outhanging, socks half-masted, messy-haired,
>> homeworkless.
>> (P.V., Cranbrook School, Sydney, Australia.)

> Did you ever see a polar bear?
> Ground-crunching, ivory-haired, thick-headed,
>> lumbering.
>> (P.S., Collins' School, Yukon, Canada.)

> Did you ever see an Opera House?
> Shining-sailed, giant-jawed, dreadfully-depleted,
>> monstrously-monied.
>> (R.H., Cranbrook School, Sydney, Australia.)

> Did you ever see a swinger?
> Nicotine-nailed, transistor-eared, sharp-shoed,
>> fuzzy-faced.
>> (A.F., Sydney High School, Sydney, Australia.)

> Did you ever see a hamlet?
> Heather-thatched, sleepy-faced, grass-covered,
>> contented.
>> (M.L., Rugby, England.)

> Did you ever see a cat?
> Highly-polished, radar-eyed, bewitched.
>> (D.S., Lower Canada College, Montreal, Canada.)

SOUND: This device is an extension of the one above and concentrates on the element of sound. As an introduction, the teacher should give a brief explanation of onomatopoeia, alliteration, and assonance. Young writers should be taught that the use of sound effect is basic to the movement of poetry.

One or two examples should be given before the pupil writes.

These begin in the same way:
> Did you ever hear a . . . .?

Suitable topics for this device might be the sounds of animals, nature, the elements, vehicles, or machines.

> Did you ever hear a sonar-beeper?
> Echo-sounding, bottom-pounding, ear-flattening,
>   ping-ponging.
>> (G.T., St. George's School, Vancouver, Canada.)

> Did you ever hear a school bus?
> Tummy-rumbling, brakes-squeaking, rock-'n-rolling.
>> (L.R., J. J. Cahill High School, Sydney, Australia.)

> Did you ever hear a brass razoo?
> Piercingly-pitched, highly-harmonized, rollickingly-
>   rhythmed.
>> (T.S., Lyndon Institute, Vermont, U.S.A.)

EZRA POUND COUPLETS

The device about to be described is introduced to help the pupil become aware of the importance of capturing the precise moment through his writing. Whenever a meaningful experience arises, he must first record it in his mind and later attempt to put it into words. The technique of capturing the moment is one which the poet must develop just as surely as the artist, or the photographer. The extent to which he is able to master this technique will, in some measure, determine the quality of his expression.

The teacher should present as his example the Ezra Pound couplet, "In a Station of the Metro":

> The apparition of these faces in the crowd;
> Petals on a wet, black bough.

He should explain that Pound wrote this couplet while standing at the exit of a subway late at night watching the travellers coming up from the darkness of the underground into the brightness of the street lights. The marked contrast of their white faces against the black background sparked the image "petals on a wet, black bough", which is concrete and visually accurate. Through it, Pound has frozen his moment of awareness and transmitted it for others to enjoy.

The pupil should be given two alternative versions of the second line, and asked to evaluate them:

"Dry leaves blown down the dry gutter."

or

"Dead leaves caught in the gutter's stream."

He should be able to recognize the inappropriateness of these latter images as compared with the first one. They miss the mark by not presenting a strong visual impact, and as such are the product both of imprecise observation, and of loose expression.

Once the aim of these Ezra Pound couplets is established, the pupil should be asked to write some containing images of his own. He may find it helpful to concentrate on a subject which has some distinctive element of movement, and attempt to stop this movement in his image:

An acrobat hanging from a tightrope;
A spider dangling from his thread.
                    (P.S., Canberra Grammar School, Australia.)

A full moon in a dark sky;
A white plate on a blue-black table cloth.
          (R.M., Melbourne Grammar School, Melbourne, Australia.)

Crumbling ruins on a craggy cliff;
A skeleton bleaching on a desert dune.
                              (R.L., Repton, England.)

A bicycle winding in and out of traffic;
A pilot fish in a school of sharks.
            (E.M., Cranbrook School, Sydney, Australia.)

Winter poplars gaunt and straight;
Old brooms in a witches' cupboard.
        (M.W., Bishop's College School, Lennoxville, Canada.)

A small tug pulling a mighty liner;
An ant dragging a twig away.
            (P.G., Horace Mann School, New York, U.S.A.)

An atomic bomb exploding on a desert;
A mushroom in a child's sandpit.
            (P.O., Lower Canada College, Montreal, Canada.)

A stream of cars going up a hill;
A column of ants climbing a wall.
                        (M.T., Eton College, England.)

The goods train plunging over a cliff;
A centipede falling off the garden wall.

(A.B., Cranbrook School, Sydney, Australia.)

THE FORM POEM

The form poem is a flexible device consisting of a series of individual words—they may be nouns, verbs, adjectives, adverbs, or any other part of speech—connected, not grammatically, but in association, and structurally separated by commas. Each stanza of a form poem assumes the following design:

```
————— , ————— , ————— , ————— ,   (A)
————— , ————— , ————— ,           (B)
————— , ————— , ————— , ————— ,   (A)
————— , ————— , ————— .           (B)
```

Thus every stanza has four lines, the first and third containing four words, the second and fourth, three. The final words of each line have an A, B, A, B rhyme scheme. No set metre or scansion is prescribed; however any effective form poem usually has some basic rhythm.

This device has the advantage for the beginner of being free from grammatical restrictions, while at the same time giving him a specific design for his subject. The skilfully constructed form poem channels the reader's mind into associative leaps not so great as to be confusing, or so small as to be meaningless. Each word must be exact for its context, and should hit its target forcefully.

My experience has been that the form poem can be used with effectiveness through the entire range of ages and abilities. I have tried it with classes of adults and university students who recognize the demands it imposes, and hence try to make each of their word choices precise. I have also introduced it to slow learners in special classes, who, if given sufficient time, find they are able to produce pleasing results with it.

The form poem may be applied to a wide variety of subjects. Its range and flexibility will become more apparent as the pupil develops experience. In type, it may be descriptive, narrative, expositional, or present a particular mood. Structurally, it may be alliterative, with all words in a line beginning with the same sound; it may represent a progression; it may be composed of lines that concentrate on a particular movement; or it may present an unusual ending or "punch" word.

In his introduction, the teacher should sketch on the board the design of the model, following this by information on its structure and use. At least three different introductions are possible: a first consists of describing the pattern of the poem without further comment, and setting the pupils to write; as a second, in addition to offering the pattern, the teacher should read a number of form poems as examples; as a third, the teacher should add to the pattern and examples an explanation of the techniques involved in the construction of any effective form poem. The able writer will understand the device without more than a brief explanation, and hence the first brief introduction should prove sufficient. In fact, he will probably find an extensive introduction a limitation on the development of his own ideas.

The slower pupil, on the other hand, may require considerable background before he can write successfully, and hence may prefer the second or third introductions proposed above. The teacher should try to present material appropriate to the ability of his class, and make modifications for individuals where possible.

PORPOISES AT NIGHT

Flickering, ghostly, splashing, deep,
Upwards, downwards, turning;
Shadows, sparkling, languid, creep,
Lurking, speeding, burning.

(G.W., St. John's School, Winnipeg, Canada.)

This piece was written by a boy who had been watching porpoises swimming through the orange beams cast by the lights in an aquarium. I have included it as an example of the effects that can be achieved through the use of words depicting movement. The slow pace of the first and third lines, representing the lethargic progress of the fish at some moments, is contrasted with the quicker pace of the second and fourth lines, representing moments of swift movement. The boy used the word "burning" because the light falling on the sides of the porpoises reminded him of matches being struck in a dark room, and he wanted to transmit this visual impression.

STEEPLECHASE

Sleepless, taut, sweating, tense,
    Call-over, start, sprint.
Muddle, spreading, tiring, fence,
    Trip, fall, splint.

(W.P., Repton, England.)

This narrative poem is included as an illustration of a "punch-word" conclusion. The young writer actually chose his ending first, and then built his rhyme scheme around it, a possibility that might be suggested to pupils in any discussion of technique.

MUSIC

Opera, viola, timpani, pop,
    Jazz, bells, brass,
Boom, bang, rattle, bop,
    Clang, squeak, crash.

(J.F., Belmont Hill School, Boston, U.S.A.)

INDUSTRY

Smoke, soot, smell, choke,
    Flash, orange, black,
Steel, iron, coal, coke,
    Truck, rails, track.

(P.V., School 52, Moscow, U.S.S.R.)

TRYING TO MILK A COW

Kick, milk, ouch, spilt,
    Bucket, swish, tail,
Stool, upright, totter, tilt,
    Hoof, stomach, wail.

(S.B., Collins' School, Yukon, Canada.)

LATIN

Amo, amas, amat, amamus,
    Bellum, bellum, belli,
Anni, annorum, mensa, annus,
    Omnibus, chasing, ME.

(J.G., Sydney Grammar School, Sydney, Australia.)

PORTA VACAT CULPA[3]

Blackboard, maps, desks, master,
    Inky, greyness, pen,
Coldness, glum, chattering, plaster,
    Dingy, Latin, den.

Ticking, Physics, compass, splodge,
    Beatings, essays, dust,
Chalk, inkpots, canes, dodge,
    Form, spelling, MUST.

(R.H., Repton, England.)

This last poem was produced in an ageing and completely un-heated classroom by a boy who had just received his half-term marks and had been placed last in his group. I include it as an illustration of being true to one's feeling at the moment of writing. The poem is a portrait of despair and has merit because it mirrors with honesty the mood of its writer.

THE SYLLABLE POEM

The syllable poem is proposed as a transitional step between the single words of the form poem and the rhythmic precision of the haiku. The pupil must count the number of syllables in each line and build up a structure with the following pattern:

Syllables

1	——
2	—— ——
3	—— —— ——
4	—— —— —— ——
5	—— —— —— —— ——
4	—— —— —— ——
3	—— —— ——
2	—— ——
1	——

The number of syllables per line increases in progression from one to five, and then back to one again. Obviously the five-syllable

[3] *Porta Vacat Culpa*, the motto of Repton School, Derbyshire, states that the school is not responsible for the shortcomings of its students; "ticking" refers to the compulsory salute that every boy must give whenever he meets a member of the staff; "splodge" is slang for any untidy mess.

line may contain either one word of five syllables, or five words of one syllable, or any other combination adding up to five.

As an introduction to this device, I have found success in making monster bubbles in class with the aid of a ring and some liquid detergent. I ask the pupils to watch the demonstration carefully and put down all the words that the colours, shapes, or movement of the bubbles suggest. They then work the best of their words into the required form and produce results such as the following:

dip
and blow
softly   now
many   bubbles
opalescent, bright
rising,   fragile
fading,   weak
white, pure
pop
(E.M., Geelong Grammar School,
Australia.)

blow
swirling
oil slick slip
flabby bulbous
bouncy wobbleful
slowly   sinking
fragile fade
going
gone
(E.M., Cranbrook School, Sydney,
Australia.)

fill
the bowl
dip the ring
wave it smoothly
snake of colour, round
giant   bubble
silver globe
fall now
drop
(M.L., Brisbane Grammar School,
Brisbane, Australia.)

out
rising
monstrous shapes
spectral   colours
oscillating   slow
wiggling downwards
soapy   drip
groundwards
splat
(P.T., Avalon Beach School,
Sydney, Australia.)

HAIKU

The haiku is a traditional form of Japanese verse, composed of three short lines of five, seven, and five syllables respectively, a total of seventeen syllables in all.

—————————— 5 (syllables)
———————————— 7 (syllables)
————————— 5 (syllables)

It is adapted to conveying atmosphere, mood, or feeling in a concise yet sensitive way. My experience has been that pupils of all ages and abilities enjoy trying the haiku because of the precision its writing demands, and the pleasing structure it gives to developing ideas. As a teaching device its benefits should be obvious: it introduces the pupil to rhythm—as he must count the syllables while writing—and it also encourages economy of statement, the essential discipline of saying much in few words.

The haiku may be written on an unlimited range of subjects, and should have thought value in addition to whatever descriptive or emotional significance it contains. The effective haiku lends itself to discussion and close scrutiny, and reveals itself to the reader much as a flower opens to the penetration of morning sunlight.

As a means of introduction, and as an illustration from which to work, the teacher should present an example of the actual stages in the construction of a haiku:

A GOODBYE

Five months since we were,	5
Last November, in summer;	7
Togetherness lost.	5

Any haiku must be grammatically correct as well as poetically genuine. Neither the thought nor the structure of this first draft is clear. Articles may have been omitted so as to make the syllable count come out correctly. The line ending with "were" is weak. Cadences should not be broken by line endings. The first version might be improved with the following adjustments:

Five long months ago,	5
One summery November,	7
Togetherness lost.	5

The meaning is now clearer; however, a colon might be added after November to substitute for what may be a missing verb, and to ease a rather abrupt transition. Further altered the haiku might read:

Five summery months ago	7
In cold November,	5
Togetherness lost.	5

In this revision, however, the syllable count violates the rules of haiku, and the meaning is again obscure. Further re-arrangement might produce the following:

> Togetherness lost,   5
> One warm November summer,   7
> Five cold months ago.   5

In this final version, cadences and endings coincide, each line finishes with a strong word, and the syllable count is accurate. The haiku is grammatically correct, poetically satisfactory, and clear in meaning, having been improved with each revision. By using this or a similar example—and perhaps even handing out copies to the pupils—the teacher should demonstrate the actual techniques involved in the writing of a haiku.

SUNRISE

Sunrise comes like paint,
Pinks and blues—watery hues,
Smudging out the night.

(T.G., Barker College, Sydney, Australia.)

SUNDAY SCHOOL

"Do unto others",
Until you are old enough
To kill Goliath.

(P.V., Repton, England.)

WATERFALL

Clear gushing water,
Slushing over shadowed rocks,
Past the damp green bank.

(M.S., The Grange School, Santiago, Chile.)

VIETNAM

Bullets race for home;
Home to them's a mother's heart;
But babes can't eat lead.

(A.S., Cranbrook School, Sydney, Australia.)

ROSES

Colours of the rainbow,
Standing on their stems of green,
Swaying with the wind.

(G.A., Shawnigan Lake School, Victoria, Canada.)

WORM

Long rippling body
Sightless, groping in the dark,
A shoe string, quite lost.

(S.M., St. Peter's College, Adelaide, Australia.)

CHIMNEYS

Chimneys reaching high
Standing like birds on one leg
Belching with no aim.

(J.A., Lower Canada College, Montreal, Canada.)

THE SCHOOL DAY

The chalk is screeching,
All the boys are whispering,
School is in progress.

(S.T., Horace Mann School, New York, U.S.A.)

THE ARTIST

Swiftly moves the brush
Quickly forms the flowing paint—
A matchless portrait.

(B.V., The Dragon School, Oxford, England.)

OLD COW

The old cow has come
To be milked and then, go out
To begin again.

(D.G., Brisbane Grammar School, Brisbane,
Australia.)

Each of these young writers found that, in a particular way, the
haiku served him well in transmitting his own feeling or idea.[4]

---

[4] For further illustrations of the haiku see Chapter 9.

COMPOSITE SEQUENCE

As a final stage in this introductory form series, I have found that pupils benefit from a review of the five different devices with which they have worked so far. I suggest to them that they select as a theme a single topic such as the sea, the desert, or the snake. They then develop this theme through each of the five stages—the Dylan Thomas portrait, Ezra Pound couplet, form poem, syllable poem, and haiku—presenting these stages in whatever sequence they feel most appropriate. The resulting composite, apart from providing a useful means of review, usually gives the pupil satisfaction, particularly if he has used each of his forms to depict a different characteristic of his theme. This assignment might best be carried out by the pupil at home as an end-of-term project. The restriction imposed by time rules against its completion within any single classroom period.

Theme: MY DOG

DYLAN THOMAS Did you ever see a Dachshund?
PORTRAIT: Long-bodied, stubby-legged, floppy-eared.

EZRA POUND COUPLET: A puppy running, jumping and barking—
A chestnut in a fire.

FORM POEM: Long, low, dark, brown,
Soft, sleek, cuddles,
Jump, bark, run, bound,
Inside, bad, puddles.

HAIKU: See the sausage dog
Standing ready near the gate
He is long indeed.

SYLLABLE POEM: Run
Jumping
Bounding high
Gobbling up flies
Mum, dad, John and I
Play with puppy
Tired at last
Kennel
Sleep

(R.P., Cranbrook School, Sydney, Australia.)

Theme: MAN'S POSITION IN LIFE

EZRA POUND COUPLET: A man running desperately . . .
An ant fleeing the heavy, careless boot.

DYLAN THOMAS
PORTRAIT: Did you ever see a big-brass general?
Stiff-upper-lipped, spit-and-polished,
crease-trousered, crease-faced.

FORM POEM: Guilty, condemned, sentence, death,
Prison, warder, stare,
Food, repentant, mercy, breath,
Walk, noose, prayer

HAIKU: Long lines of people
Always rushing to and fro
Stop, crazy people

SYLLABLE POEM: Clang
Bell rings
People stand
Many   voices
Children packing books
Feet are trudging
Going   home
Happy
Now
(P.L., Canberra High School, Australia.)

Theme: THE STORM

HAIKU: The might of Nature,
Spectacularly unleashed,
A thundering crash.

EZRA POUND COUPLET: Black clouds covering the sky;
An ink stain slowly spreading.

DYLAN THOMAS
PORTRAIT: Did you ever see a rainstorm?
Overwhelmingly-drenching, thunderously-noisy,
irresistibly-powerful.

SYLLABLE POEM:

I
was caught
in the fields
by the rainstorm
I ran for shelter
Puffing, gasping;
The first drops
Came down:
drenched.

FORM POEM: Darken, ominous, rumble, clouds,
Drip, patter, hissed,
Rain, fall, curtain, shroud,
Slacken, stop, mist

(G.T., Harrow School, England.)

CHAPTER 3

CONTENT CATEGORIES

"What shall I write about?" This is one of the main questions facing any pupil about to attempt a poem. If he chooses a subject that is significant to him—whether it be diesel engines, hamburgers, or broken window panes—then his chances of success should be increased. Otherwise, he is unlikely to produce anything genuine and his expression will ring false.

To what extent should a teacher be guided in his choice of material by what his pupils like or understand at the moment? The expression "They like it" may mean no more than that it is familiar or easy. The real reward for the pupil occurs when he is brought to appreciate things which previously were new, and perhaps even strange. If he is fed exclusively on a diet of what he already enjoys and can grasp without effort, he will eventually be reduced to boredom. Hence the role of the teacher should be that of a guide who presents suggestions which will enable every pupil to discover inspiration and new meaning for himself.

In the following pages there are three different categories of subject matter: sources of inspiration, sensory stimuli, and themes from the arts. Each teacher should treat these as a starting point in building an ever wider list of suggestions.

SOURCES OF INSPIRATION

The following general themes are presented as a guide for the teacher:

ACTIVITIES
Work   School—subjects, clubs, travel.
                        Community—church, scouts, social.
                        Vacation jobs.

Play	Sports—experiences, descriptions, goals.
	Hobbies—aims, pleasures.
	Recreation—leisure hours, thought.
Special occasions	Travel—trips, visits.
	Holidays—celebrations, parties.
	Experiences—actual, imaginary.

SURROUNDINGS

Immediate	Home—room, garden, neighbourhood.
	School—classroom, facilities, features.
Geographical	Town or city—life, sights.
	Nation or world—patriotism, internationalism.
Natural	Physical features—sky, sea, mountains, sun, stars.
	Country—farms, fields, crops, life.
	Flora—trees, plants, flowers.
	Fauna—animals, birds, fish, pets.
	Elements—weather, seasons, day, night.

REFLECTIONS

Issues of our time	Space—The Bomb, planets, jets.
	Human welfare—poverty, prejudice, war, protest.
	Communication—advertising, TV, literature.
Personal concerns	Relationships with others—family, friends.
	Hopes—aims, dreams, future.
	Fears—security, conformity, identity.

From among the general topics outlined above, any number of more specific themes can be developed. As an illustration, three particular possibilities are suggested:

Fauna (from the section above on natural surroundings): An attempt should be made to propose a novel subject and link it with an original approach. Fauna such as the moth, fly, cobra, jaguar, or tortoise might provide fresh inspiration for the pupil, who should be asked to concentrate on minute details and movements after the manner of Walter de la Mare.[1] This focus should

[1] This approach should be linked with the exercises on scale outlined later in this chapter.

enable pupils to create pieces such as the following by a boy who noticed an unusual subject:

THE GRUB
Creeping through the grass,
With sharp and spiny bristles;
This segmented grub.
(R.R., The Dragon School, Oxford, England.)

The City (from the section above on regional surroundings): Attention might be directed to such themes involving the city as change, mystery, movement, or industrial elegance. Variety can be achieved by concentrating on buildings (old, new, skyscrapers, memorial), activities (men and machines at work, traffic circulation, and noise), or other centres of interest (sites, occupations, colours, and movements). The following piece presents an unusual aspect of the city:

CITY STREET ON A RAINY NIGHT
Busy traffic splashes by;
Exhaust fumes cut the heavy air;
Neon lights flash double bright;
I feel security in the glare.
(P.S., The Hill School, San Francisco, U.S.A.)

The Weather (from the section above on natural surroundings): All living things are natural barometers and change as the weather changes. Mood depends on the weather, and elements such as the wind, the rain, the fog, and the mist should provide a ready source of inspiration for young writers. Who has not stood on an open hillside while the wind tore at his clothes, or huddled under cover of shelter while the rain pelted against the window panes? The weather has varied faces, and pupils should take pleasure in recalling them and derive benefit from using them as material for their poems.

MIST
Silence hangs heavy;
Nothing but the cold wind swirls,
Sweeping the white hills.
(N.B., Cranbrook School, Sydney, Australia.)

Each of the above categories becomes more meaningful by being made more specific. The following list contains a number of specific topics. It is only a short introductory list however, and teachers should add to it in consultation with their pupils:

ACTIVITIES:

Myself in a dark room feeling for the light switch.
Myself under an umbrella in a strong wind.
Myself doing an oil painting.
Myself crawling through tall grass.
Myself in pain from a splinter.
Myself jumping from a height.
Myself teaching my brother to swim.
Myself inching up the creaking stairs by candlelight.
Myself behind a fast boat on water skis.
Myself washing my hair in the shower.
Myself stuck in an elevator.
Myself visiting a fortune-teller in a gipsy caravan.
Man lighting his pipe in a dark room.
A very old lady fumbling for a key in her purse.
Boy on crutches going for a bus
Wreckers demolishing a building.
A cheerleader strutting in front of the brass band.
Woman shelling peas into a small pot.
Child reading comfortably in a soft chair.
Circus doctor examining a cut on a lion's paw.
Two boys in a speeding billy-cart.
Mother and friend having afternoon tea.
The dentist drilling a tooth.
A foal walking for the first time.
Parrots screaming at each other from adjoining cages.
Kitten playing with a ball of wool.
A driver racing a sports car around a circuit.
Giraffe eating leaves from a tree.
Two men carrying a heavy bundle.
Vendors selling balloons at the carnival.
The table at Christmas dinner.
The parking lot of a supermarket at noon.
Policeman lecturing three boys.
Crowd at the beach on a sunny afternoon.
The dormitory after lights-out.
A boy trying to eat rice with chopsticks.

SURROUNDINGS:

The barnyard at daybreak.
An apple tree in blossom.
Fireworks exploding in the night sky.
Surf breaking against the cliff.
Sounds of a Grand Prix motor race.
The view from the top of a skyscraper.
The classroom just after the teacher leaves.
The bush at sunset.
Wind in the branches.
Spanish bull-ring on Saturday afternoon.
Lightning striking a gum tree.
A piece of ground before and after a bulldozer goes over it.
Icicles hanging from a drain-pipe.
A downtown street at night.
The bargain counter during a sale.
A lighthouse beam shining on wet rocks.
Smoke rising from an autumn fire.
A revolving door at rush hour.

REFLECTIONS:

Child shivering on a doorstep.
Soft peach being peeled.
Clown singing to the accompaniment of a ukulele.
The family window-shopping.
A flock of starlings sitting on a telegraph wire.
An elephant wallowing in a mud bath.
Leaf floating down a river.
Three men plotting a scheme.
The fin of a shark gliding through the water.
A crowd of young people listening to a jazz concert.
A cat stalking a sparrow.
Night sounds in the woods.
A man who never smiles.
Boy playing the bagpipes.
Captain on the bridge of his ship.
A skeleton bleaching on the desert.
An astronaut in a space capsule.
Frost patterns on the window pane.

SENSORY STIMULI

The stimuli in this section appeal to each of the five senses, and have been grouped for ease of reference. The teacher should use the suggestions in conjunction with any of the form stages he feels appropriate.

SIGHT

Scale: The element of scale can be used to provide the pupil with a different dimension from which to write. He should be asked to gaze intently at some small object such as a piece of Eskimo soapstone carving, and to imagine that he is growing smaller and smaller while the object is growing correspondingly larger. The effect of this experiment can be startling, and generally enables him to produce something with an unusual perspective:

THE ANT

See the towering ant,
Pushing mighty forests down,
He is not afraid.

(P.V., The Grange School, Santiago, Chile.)

The boy wrote his poem while lying face down in the grass watching a number of ants move through the blades.

Another pupil described his sensation at seeing a moth lying partly drowned on the wet ground after a heavy rainstorm:

THE MOTH

I walk up nearer and squat down
To take a closer look;
I see a massive aeroplane,
Its wreckage in a brook.

(D.W., Scotch College, Perth, Australia.)

I have found success in using this approach out of doors with almost any small subject from nature, or in the classroom with objects such as a piece of coloured stone or a pine cone.

The element of scale may also be used in reverse by asking the pupil to imagine that he is growing larger while his subject—preferably of considerable size to begin with—becomes progressively smaller.

Order out of chaos: In this section, the pupil should be asked to study various unrelated objects arranged on a tray, such as a magnifying glass, a paper clip, an orange, a knife, and a used train ticket. He is required to associate two or more of the objects in writing a poem. All creation involves artistic choice, and making associations under varied conditions exercises the imagination, and develops flexibility of expression.

The pupil might likewise be shown a photograph composed of a number of unusual or disjointed elements and be required to unify them in making a poem. He might also inspect an object such as a bowl of fruit, a Ubangi native doll, or a model sailing ship and be asked to produce a definite reaction to it.

This Australian pupil, confronted with a large colour photograph of an Aboriginal ritual, produced an unusual piece of order-out-of-chaos:

CORROBOREE

Wheeling, whirling, ducking, leaping,
Yells, cries, chants,
Writhing, weaving, crawling, creeping,
Fight? hunt? dance!

(S.T., Scotch College, Melbourne, Australia.)

SOUND

Response to a single effect: The pupil should be presented with a sound stimulus as he sits in class and then asked to write something evoked by the sound that he hears. He should keep his eyes closed in order to heighten his concentration on the effect itself. Before presenting the actual stimulus, the teacher should review various sound devices such as alliteration, assonance and onomatopoeia, perhaps even presenting some exercises to help the pupil to recall them. The young writer should then be expected to make use of sound words in constructing his poem. Any of the following, whether presented live, or on record, should elicit a reaction: splintering glass, a teletype machine, racing cars at full throttle, footsteps, chalk screeching on the blackboard, or the distant whistle of a train.

This boy wrote a response to a recording of the simulated sounds of a mediaeval battle:

AGINCOURT

Canter, gallop, trot, clash,
   Cut, clang, groan,
Screaming, swinging, buckle, smash,
   Whinnying, sighing, moan.

(A.L., Lower Canada College, Montreal, Canada.)

Order out of chaos: The pupil should be asked to associate combinations of auditory stimuli much as he was asked to inter-relate visual ones in the section above. Emphasis is placed on exercising artistic choice and developing some pattern between unrelated effects. The teacher should present sounds on tape in some pre-arranged order, repeating the sequence a number of times over. The following combinations might be useful:

1. Bells—sleigh, school, cow, church, wedding.
2. Warning sirens—foghorn, ship's whistle, ambulance, fire alarm.
3. Animals—tiger, dingo, mouse, gorilla, elephant.
4. Jazz concert—trumpet, drums, guitar, xylophone.

This pupil was captivated by the sounds of a jazz concert as he wrote:

TIJUANA TAXI

Trumpet, guitar, drum, bass,
   Blow, pluck, clash,
Brass, twang, wheeling, pace,
   Racket, horn, smash.

(P.T., Horace Mann School, New York, U.S.A.)

FEELING

Texture: The teacher should ask the pupils to keep their eyes closed while they feel some object being passed around the room. They should be required to describe the nature of the object they have felt without naming it, but by alluding to its texture only. This exercise should prove more effective if the teacher is able to bring a number of objects to the class, and give one to each row. A type of contest should then be held as all the pupils in the same row read poems about their object, and pupils in the other rows attempt to guess its identity from the pieces they have heard. A number of objects should prove suitable for this approach: a cake of soap, a sponge, a piece of plasticine, a pincushion, a seashell, or a powder puff.

This boy from the north of Canada wrote a haiku in response to an object with which he was familiar:

THE ICICLE
Feel the chilling spear,
Sending shivers through my hand,
Cold and glacial knife.
(P.T., Collins' School, Yukon, Canada.)

Physical sensations: The pupil should be asked to recall some strenuous physical activity, and to describe the sensations he experienced at the time. The teacher should give him some general questions as a guide to his recollection:

Exactly what feeling did you have in your limbs?
Did you feel tired, breathless, heavy, light-headed?
Was there a sensation of heat or cold involved?
Did you tremble, or shiver, or feel tense?

Situations such as the following should prove suitable: swimming underwater, riding a bicycle at high speed downhill, climbing a rope, or running in a school mile.

As a variation of the above suggestion, the pupil might be asked to submit himself to some physical experience such as standing outside in the cold, sprinting uphill, rolling a boulder along the ground, or skipping. He should record his sensations of the moment as the basis for his later expression.

This Australian boy recalled his experiences in the school swimming sports:

THE HUNDRED YARDS
Tension, blocks, cramps, inhaling,
Straining, gun, splash,
Gliding, gasping, thrashing, flailing,
Sprint, exhaustion, crash.
(P.G., Newington College, Sydney, Australia.)

SMELL: In this section, the pupil, again with his eyes closed, should be presented with various smells, and asked to produce a response to them. Describing his reaction with any accuracy is a difficult task, particularly if he is trying to transmit it so that others may have a similar experience. The teacher should select smells which will pervade the whole classroom such as sulphur, bottled kitchen seasonings, perfume, camphor, or honeysuckle.

EGGS
Acrid sulphur smell,
Bites my nose and makes me reel,
Pungent, rotten eggs.
(W.B., Charterhouse, England.)

TASTE: The same principles apply to this sense as to the others already mentioned. The teacher will probably find it more difficult to use in the classroom, however. If offering actual taste sensations such as leeks, bacon, lemon, or peppermint proves impracticable, then the pupil will have to use his memory. Alternatively, he could be asked to do some taste research at home, and come prepared for the next writing session.

CURRY
One taste sears the throat,
Decapitates the tastebuds,
Solid knock-out gas.

Spewing forth foul stench,
Plays havoc with my nostrils,
I'm left here gasping.
(E.M., Cranbrook School, Sydney, Australia.)

THEMES FROM THE ARTS
The material in this section is taken from three different fields: literature, art, and movement. In Chapter Six the themes will be extended to include sculpture, music, and drama.

The Arts should provide a ready source of inspiration for those who are aware of their potential. The teacher should use the themes suggested here as stimuli with any of the form stages for which he feels they are suited.

LITERATURE: All writing, no matter how original it may appear, is to some degree imitative. The work that any pupil does is a product, in part at least of what he has read and experienced. He can say, like Tennyson's Ulysses: "I am a part of all that I have met." Consequently, the teacher should try to introduce his pupils to some of the best of their literary heritage. He should read several carefully chosen pieces of prose and poetry as an introduction to a writing session. For instance, if he wants his pupils to think about the sea, he might read a prose section from Conrad's *Nigger of the Narcissus*, and follow this with Masefield's poems "Cargoes" and "Sea Fever". He should use these pieces as teaching devices in pointing out effective examples of word usage, and commenting on other poetic effects and how they are achieved. Such a background from the teacher should help the pupil to write about his subject with understanding.

The following poem offers an illustration of vivid imagery. It focuses on various animals in their sweltering cages at the zoo:

> The apes yawn and adore their fleas in the sun.
> The parrots shriek as if they were on fire, or strut
> Like cheap tarts to attract the stroller with the nut.
> Fatigued with indolence, tiger and lion
> Lie still as the sun. The boa-constrictor's coil
> Is a fossil. Cage after cage seems empty, or
> Stinks of sleepers from the breathing straw.
> It might be painted on a nursery wall.[2]

After hearing this example, three pupils in the same class produced these poems, each one about an animal, and each distinctive in its own way:

THE CAT

The cat shimmers black
Like cold nights
In the middle of winter.
Its teeth shine white;
Its tail lies long;
How sly it is.

(D.H., Repton, England.)

THE SPIDER

Spider, legs, spinning, eight,
House, people, cat,
Creeping, inching, red-back, fate,
Man, slipper, splat.

(P.T., Repton, England.)

2 These are the first eight lines of the poem "Jaguar", by Ted Hughes.

THE SNAKE

Slithering through grass,
Searching in a silent way,
Careless mouse, beware!

(M.M., Repton, England.)

ART: The teacher should assemble for presentation to his classes a series of visual stimuli such as paintings and designs. These stimuli should be offered in a sequence that moves from the traditional to the less conventional. For example, if paintings are being shown, the teacher should start with landscapes, portraits, and scenes that are easily interpreted, before moving to more complex or abstract work. In this way he builds the confidence of the pupil by progressing from the known to the less familiar. The pupil may want to begin with abstract or impressionist work but if he is allowed to do so, he may become confused with problems of interpretation in addition to those of clear written expression. The more concrete the visual stimulus, the less temptation the pupil should have to ramble in thought and word.

This boy derived inspiration from a close study of da Vinci's portrait of the Mona Lisa:

LEONARDO'S LAMENT

Fair buxom beauty which the world adores,
That secret smirk of woman's confidence,
I love all this, my Mona Lisa.

The long smooth hair, like coffee freshly brewed,
Those downy kid-gloved hands clasped to her side;
I love all this, my Mona Lisa.

And she will sit there dreaming out at us,
For all the years that men can count from now;
But she is dead, my Lisa love.

(A.S., Cranbrook School, Sydney, Australia.)

In addition to using pieces of art, the teacher might present such other visual stimuli as a dollar note, a road map, or a piece of old newspaper. He should offer more than one item in each writing session so that every pupil is given a chance to see a subject that interests him.

MOVEMENT: The area of movement is one with which the pupil will already be familiar through physical education and games. An understanding of the potential of this medium, however, can lead to the practice of writing from the inside out. Let me explain. The teacher should compile a list of subjects, each involving some distinctive action, and ask the pupil to move as the subject might. For example, the pupil might create through his body movements a simulation of a palm tree in the wind or of an octopus on the ocean floor.

The exercise is intended principally as a means of letting the pupil experience a subject from the inside, hence making it more realistic. The teacher should take the pupils to some secluded part of the school grounds and there ask them to close their eyes, concentrate on his suggestions, and move to them in an uninhibited way. For the first few suggestions the pupils will probably be stiff and somewhat uneasy, but realizing that nobody is watching them, they should soon become relaxed and genuinely enjoy the experience.

Any of the following sequences should prove successful to the pupil who is concentrating on them:

Sea
Palm tree in the wind
Field of beach grass
Shark swimming through water
Scuba diver
Sailboat in a breeze
Wave rolling onto shore
Jellyfish floating on surface
Undersea plant in the current

Animals
Tiger stalking his prey
Hippo in a mud bath
Frog catching flies
Chick just out of the shell
Bull in the ring
Seal in the zoo
Wolf baying at the moon
Cat sleeping on a cushion

Objects
Folding chair
Neon sign flashing
Stepladder against wall
Mechanical wind-up toy
Typewriter
Wheelbarrow
Paintbrush on canvas
Vacuum cleaner

Activities
Policeman directing traffic
Acrobat on a tight-rope
Surfer on a board
Matador in the ring
Juggler doing a stunt
Mountain climber using ropes
Racing driver in cockpit
Conductor leading the orchestra

Motion

Candle slowly burning
Flag waving on staff
Swan flying in sunset
Astronaut weightless in space
Orchid opening to sun
Fountain flowing with water
Fire dying down
Rubber tyre blown up, down

A movement sequence should last for from five to seven minutes, after which the pupil should be asked to write about any of the suggestions he has found exciting. If he does not feel like writing on the spot, however, he should relax and simply think about the experience. Immediate results are not important. The lasting value of this exercise is that the pupil, once having become involved in any subject, can use this experience to imagine any number of additional situations at any time in the future. Although he may never have tried being a snake slithering through the grass, if he is asked to write a poem or piece of prose on the snake, his imagination should enable him to do so. He can thus create an atmosphere of realism for himself, and hence write from the inside out.

I suggest that teachers do no more than two movement sequences with any one class. The exercise should not be used to provide a regular direct source of inspiration.

The following poem was produced by a thirteen-year-old boy immediately after he had taken part in a movement sequence in which one of the subjects I suggested was a fire starting, burning brightly, and then dying. He wrote it in ten minutes, and with little difficulty. As he handed it in he said: "I could never have written this yesterday." This perhaps best illustrates the value, for most pupils, of the approach of writing from the inside out.

THE FIRE

A grey whisper twists up from the pile of leaves;
Tentacles of smoke ooze from between the branches;
Suddenly orange flames spring out;
Twigs and ferns blacken and crumple;
Wisps of ash lift and swirl in the shimmering air;

A bough falls in myriads of sparks;
The flames lick hungrily around it.
With a final flare the log collapses in fiery fragments;
Against the bright curtain of fire,
Tiny black specks spiral upwards.
Finally, there are just a few dark glowing chunks,
And some white ash fluttering away in the breeze.

(C.L., Cranbrook School, Sydney, Australia.)

CHAPTER 4

EVALUATION EXERCISES

Shortly after he has written his first few poems every pupil should be asking himself at least two important questions: Are my pieces of any value? How can I improve my writing? Guidelines are presented here which should be of help to any young writer in assessing his own progress and improving his technique.

If this strand of the programme is to be useful, evaluation must be considered as a positive and constructive force. It must be regarded not as an exercise in tearing down, but as one in understanding how a poem is put together, how it is built up.

Neither should the process of evaluation be rushed or introduced until the pupil is ready for it. He must first have written a number of poems, experienced an enjoyment yet felt an inadequacy, and hence have a desire to improve his expression. When evaluation comes as a result of this felt need, then its introduction is natural and its effects are constructive.

It is important for teachers to treat the first written efforts of their pupils with understanding. Whenever a beginner shows me a piece that is of little significance by any mature standard, I am careful not to belittle it. Rather I try to pick out any bright parts it contains—even if they are only a few words—and praise him for these. If he has given me his trust by trying to write something, I owe him the respect of encouragement, and should attempt to nurture his interest.

By the same token, I am responsible for providing the criteria of evaluation which will help him to develop standards and a discriminating taste. The training of his critical faculties should increase his understanding and enjoyment of all poetry.

Some pupils may believe that there are no "right answers" in English, and that expression is largely a matter of feeling. They approach their Science subjects with care, and take the exact steps required to arrive at a geometrical Q.E.D. Nonetheless they consider that English requires no such precise approach—after all it is the language they speak, and therefore they should be able to write it with little attention to detail.

Writing effectively is just as much a science as it is an art. Definite standards of expression can be established. It is the responsibility of every English teacher, firstly to know and understand these standards, and secondly to transmit them to his pupils.

The pupil must catch a similar spirit. He must seek "right answers" and be uncompromising in setting standards for himself. If he is presented with sound criteria of assessment he will soon be able to make valid judgments. In fact, his evaluation of any poem may often be more genuine than that of the adult critic because he comes to it without expectations or preconceptions. The young writer has a natural inclination to appreciate sincerity, and is quick to recognize it.

I shall now present evaluation exercises and suggestions under four headings: initial criteria of judgment, constructive criticism, personal assessment, and a framework for evaluation. These exercises should be done during actual writing periods, and in conjunction with other aspects of the programme.

INITIAL CRITERIA OF JUDGMENT

The main difficulty facing any beginner attempting to evaluate a poem is his uncertainty about the criteria of judgment he should use. I have found that if he is given several leading questions as a framework for his assessment, he proceeds with more confidence than if he is simply asked to write without direction.

In the early stages, the young writer will not know what to look for in a poem. Consequently I propose three areas of consideration for him. Each of these is accompanied by a question which he answers by giving a simple "yes" or "no" reply, and a brief sentence or two of qualification. As he progresses, he should find his assessments easier and his judgments more meaningful, since they will be based on experience. He should ask himself these three questions:

CONTENT: Has the writer really said anything?

Under this heading, he must consider the subject matter of the poem, and what he has got from it. He might devote a sentence or so to such elements as originality and sincerity.

TECHNIQUE: Has the writer expressed himself adequately?

He should consider such aspects as choice of words, use of images, and rhythm of the poem. Again, a sentence or two on each aspect will be sufficient.

IMPACT: Has the writer got his point forcefully across to you?

Under this heading he must consider aspects of communication and response, his general impression of the poem, and whether or not it was successful for him. It is important that he be sincere in his comments, and that he does not hesitate to express his honest assessment.

At this early stage, the teacher should not expect anything sophisticated in the way of comment. He should propose these questions as a framework only, and as the criteria by which his pupils may become better informed about poetry. Honesty of response is the element which he should encourage above all others.

CONSTRUCTIVE CRITICISM

After he has developed experience in the use of these questions, the pupil should be given examples of inferior writing and asked to criticize them constructively. He must be taught to distinguish the marks of mediocre production such as: a lack of sincerity and originality; an inappropriate use of words, or abundance of clichés and trite phrases; a lack of conciseness; a tone which somehow rings false.

As a test of his judgment, the pupil might be asked to give a rating to any poem, the rating being based on the criteria suggested above. He might then compare his assessment with those of his classmates and be prepared to explain or defend his judgment.

The aim of this exercise is to give the pupil a type of lesson in reverse: he concentrates on technique by analysing how *not* to write. Sources of inferior production should be plentiful, whether they be found in poetry, journalese, hackneyed phrases, magniloquence, or diffuse prose expression. Any pupil should be able to recognize the deliberately humorous artificiality in a piece such as the following:

A THOUGHT

I wish I were a bumble bee
So merry blythe and gay
To buzz and hum from flower to flower,
All on a summer's day.

I wish I were a butterfly
Upon a buttercup;
I'd flutter down the woodland paths,
And then I'd flutter up.

I wish I were—but then, oh dear,
A sudden thought strikes me,
For if I were a butterfly,
I could not be a bee.

I'd love to be a bumble bee
All summer time and so,
I'm glad I'm not a butterfly
To flutter to and fro.

It is this sort of doggerel which debases poetry in the eyes of young readers, and which has given rise, for many, to the feeling that poetry is "for the birds". The teacher cannot destroy this heresy too quickly.

PERSONAL ASSESSMENT

Once a pupil has had some experience with the works of others, he should be better prepared to evaluate his own writing. An important aspect of this programme is that the pupil is asked to assess his work at every stage, and in so doing to become constructively critical of it. Everyone is to a certain degree blinded by his own material, and hence incapable of objective judgment. Nevertheless, there are benefits to be derived from any attempt at evaluation, even if it must be partly unsuccessful.

The pupil should write a prose comment after each of his poems, recording it below the poem itself on the right-hand page of his special exercise book. In this comment he should mention such points as how he chose his subject, what effects he attempted, what success he felt he achieved, and what he learned from his attempt. Perhaps these comments from two pupils will help to illustrate this approach:

My experience has shown me that a useful method for determining the hyphenated words in Dylan Thomas portraits is to construct prose sentences about my subject and then take words from them. For example, I was recently making a portrait of a rhinoceros and put down: "He has flanks as hard as steel." No sooner had I written this sentence than the word I was looking for jumped into my mind: "steel-flanked".

(L.G., Charterhouse, England.)

This boy had learned an important lesson as he wrote:

My poem on mountain climbing is a poor effort, I think, for never did I really feel or believe what I was writing. I chose to write on the climber yet only twice did I actually describe him. The rest is invented as I have never done any climbing. The poem isn't satisfying to me because it doesn't represent a real experience.

(J.D., Lower Canada College, Montreal, Canada.)

The pupil should be given an opportunity to evaluate his own work, not only at the end of the period in which he produces it, but also after every three or four writing sessions when poems done earlier have been allowed to grow cold. Assessment is often more valid after a lapse of time.

This exercise should be extended to include a consideration by each young writer of the work of other members of his class. Providing that the attitude of the pupils is positive, considerable benefit can result.

A FRAMEWORK FOR EVALUATION

As a later extension of the section on initial criteria of judgment, the pupil should be given a more complete series of critical questions. These should provide him with guidelines for assessing the poetry that he reads and writes. He should answer the questions in each of the three categories, using them as the basis for increasing his understanding of the poem under review:

CONTENT: Has the writer really said anything?

Originality:	Has he combined thoughts, feelings or words in a new way?
	Has he shown insight or imagination?
Sincerity:	Has he given an honest interpretation of an experience, feeling or idea?
	Is there significance for the writer in what he is trying to say?

TECHNIQUE: Has the writer expressed himself adequately?

Diction:	Is his choice of words original, appropriate, and accurate?
Imagery:	Does he use figurative language which is evocative and precise?
Structure:	Is his form effective and appropriate?
	Are the rhythm and sound movement fitting?
	Does he maintain unity of pattern, point of view, and mood?

IMPACT: Has the writer got his point across forcefully?

Communication:	Has he expressed his ideas simply, lucidly and comprehensively?
Response:	Has he evoked a reaction from the reader?

The exercises suggested in this chapter should help the pupil to develop taste in his reading, provide him with training in the techniques of effective expression, and prepare him for the more advanced form stages about to be presented.

Part II
ADVANCED

CHAPTER 5

FORM STAGES

The pupil, having completed the three introductory stages of the programme, should now be ready to try its advanced exercises. This chapter will lead him from single-line statements through metrical patterns and experimental structures to eventual freedom of form. Each stage is designed to give him greater choice of structure as he becomes more experienced with different approaches. The pupil enjoys having a specific structural model—such as the haiku—for each writing session. He then knows by the end of the period whether he has achieved his goal, and has definite criteria against which to measure his success.

We underestimate young writers if we believe that their chief difficulty lies in finding something to say. Most of them have a reservoir of subject material not far below the surface. The teacher must provide the vehicle through which they may release their ideas and feelings. In this respect the task of the teacher is similar to that of the prospector who drills for oil. Once he finds the appropriate shaft he is able to "release" the oil lying just below the ground, enabling it to come freely to the surface. I have found that the shaft providing this release is the *form* which is used. This form provides the structure through which the pupil can organize the feelings within him, which otherwise might not come to light.

COMPLETED IMAGE VARIATIONS

I shall present four variations in this section, each one giving the pupil a line framework of definite structure. He must complete every image within a single line, in this way producing a poem of self-contained statements. The advantage of this approach is that it offers the young writer a definite structure for his expression, and discourages him from stylistic flights which may obscure what he is trying to say.

CHINESE INTRODUCTION: In this first variation, the pupil should be given a model of Chinese poetry translated by Arthur Waley, Ezra Pound or any other specialist in the field. Such books as the following should prove useful: *The White Pony; an Anthology of Chinese Poetry*, Payne, R. (ed.), New York, Mentor, 1960; *The Penguin Book of Chinese Verse*, Davis, A. R. (ed.), London, Penguin Books Ltd., 1964. A distinctive characteristic of these Chinese translations is that in them the poet completes images within one line, much as the artist completes a figure with a single stroke of his brush.

The pupil should be given a model and asked to compose something similar himself. No restrictions of metre and rhyme should be imposed, however, the lines of the poem should be grammatically independent and of approximately the same length. The following piece by Tu Fu might be used as an illustration:

SUMMER NIGHT[1]

Cool perfume of bamboo pervades my room;
Wild moonlight fills the whole courtyard;
Drop by drop falls the crystal dew;
One by one the moving stars appear.
The fleeting glow-worms sparkle in dark corners;
The waterfowl on the river bank call to one another;
Everything in the world follows the path of war;
I sit on my bed meditating through the long night.

Each line of "Summer Night" contains a completed-image statement which, except for the last two lines, appeals directly to one of the senses. Before the pupil begins to write, he should make a plan of the order in which he is going to present his senses. For example, if he is planning a four-image poem on his favourite meal, he might begin with a line-statement on sight, then one on sound, then one on smell, and conclude with his strongest one, that of taste.

[1] This piece is taken from *The White Pony*, p. 195.

The following first draft of a poem by a young boy might be used to demonstrate this approach:

The moonlight streams on the water;
Shadows loom from behind tall trees;
Birds are singing their evening lullaby;
A low insistent chorus of gnats blankets the evening;
Once foiled, they swoop again upon the unsuspecting rowers.

The oar strikes the water with a slap;
The boat glides through an embroidery of leaves.
A mother duck disturbs her sleeping brood;
She quacks crossly from the farther bank;
A water rat streaks hurriedly from our path.

(D.G., The Dragon School, Oxford, England.)

This is a piece of expression on which the pupil can work with profit. As it is a first draft only, he should realize a number of points before attempting his revision.

The third line of the first verse contributes very little: "Birds" is the only working word, and the whole expression is trite and vague. The last line of the verse is untrue. Any rower already besieged by gnats is far from unsuspecting. The other images in the first verse are strong because of the use of the verbs "streams", "loom" and "blankets".

The first two lines of the second verse are telling because the image has really been seen and felt. The remainder of the verse is weakened because the words lack originality. The moonlight, trees and gnats have been directly observed. Contrast these with the expressions "sleeping brood", and the "birds' evening lullaby" which smack more of subconsciously remembered reading than of personal experience. Armed with this fuller understanding, the pupil should be able to rewrite the piece with more impact than he achieved originally.

An important element of effective expression is reserve. Young writers, particularly if they have had little training, often get carried away by words. For example, if they are asked to do something on war, they delight in spilling blood three feet deep on the floor. Unless this inclination is discouraged, they may feel that exaggeration is a mark of good writing.

The piece that follows was composed by a boy who led more than twenty thousand pupils in a New South Wales English examination. Notice the economy of his expression, and the way in which he has combined his words to produce striking images:

THE DESERT BY NIGHT

Cold moonlight steals across the stretching sand;
A dingo shatters silence with his cry;
The dark gums stand alone against the sky;
The empty night waits fearfully for morning.

(O.P., Sydney Grammar School, Sydney, Australia.)

In the following poem the writer, a boy from the slowest stream of his age group, has made an effort to come to grips with words through his use of "cataracts", "polished" and "watery":

SPRING MORNING

The morning wakes in cataracts of colour;
A stream falls into a pond of polished lilies;
The thrush emits a watery whistle;
Only the blind can see them all.

(P.R., Repton, England.)

This writer has used repetition as a device to create the atmosphere of an unpaved Canadian prairie road on a rainy autumn day:

THE ROAD

Flat and monotonous stretches the muddy road;
Silos are filled with late-summer grain;
Fences lie low and straight as railway tracks;
Flat and monotonous stretches the gravel road.

(P.V., St. John's, Ravenscourt, Winnipeg, Canada.)

This young Russian writer was impressed by the unusual elegance of an industrial scene, and has transmitted it with effectiveness in a language which is not his own:

BUILDING

Shining shafts of steel stand against the glare;
Helmeted workmen labour through the noise;
Fine dust mixes with the fresh smell of mortar;
The construction goes on all through the day.

(R.V., School 52, Moscow, U.S.S.R.)

A Malayan girl found the completed image form suitable for describing a scene which she recalled from her own country:

MALAYA

The golden rays pour down the kampong like fire;
The tall straight trees never a movement show;
Malay huts on stilts stand rigid against the sky;
Evergreen trees make my heart glow.

(A.H., Cheltenham Girls' High School, Sydney, Australia.)

PRECISE SKELETON: The pupil should be asked to build a skeleton for his completed images by establishing a specific focus for each line. For example, if a pupil wishes to write about a spider, he might establish a framework of five different aspects of his subject as follows: the first impression that comes to mind about the spider; its body; its web; its characteristic actions; and a concluding feeling or emotional response to the spider.

By preparing a framework for his writing, the pupil establishes specific points of view for his images, and hence a design for his poem.

This boy developed the skeleton outlined on the left, and then produced the following portrait of a winter machine:

THE SNOWBLOWER

(Sense)

Sound	Distant whines reveal its presence;
Sight	Its churning teeth slash at snow;
Taste	A gasping mouth spits frozen slush;
Touch	Chained paws grip the ice;
Sight	Its tail lingers in greasy smoke.

(D.S., Lower Canada College, Montreal, Canada.)

CONTRAST: In this section, the teacher should give the pupil a model and some specific goal to achieve. In keeping with his role as a practising poet, the teacher might here present one of his own poems, asking that his pupils follow a similar pattern.

MIDNIGHT FOG ON NEW COLLEGE GARDEN

Now creeps the hooded Arctic fog into cheerless refuges;
A beam, with phosphorescent fingers, searches the dumb
    recesses of the wall;
Dank vapours chill the bone of the muffled traveller;
His heart glows through the enveloping shroud.

                    (B.P., New College, Oxford.)

I wrote this poem on a bleak December night, after returning to my unheated "digs" through dank winter fog. The external situation as I groped along the old city wall was depressing. In the first three images I tried to portray this bleak external situation, and to contrast it in the final image with my feeling of inner contentment. The poem revolves around the word "glows", and represents an attempt to capture the external-internal contrast.

I do not claim poetic distinction for the piece! I have found it useful, however, in presenting a specific aim to pupils. I ask them to think of a similar situation from their own experience, and to develop a contrast for themselves.

The following poem was written by an Australian boy whose home is in New Guinea. He produced a different type of contrast in response to this introduction:

VOLCANIC LAKE IN NEW GUINEA

Its sunken blackness is encircled by stark rock above;
A noiseless calm haunts an icy sky;
I plunge through the cold harshness of iron water;
A hundred black faces are white with laughter.

          (D.H., Geelong Grammar School, Australia.)

FREE RANGE: In this fourth variation, free choice of subject matter should be given to the young writer who should be sufficiently familiar with the completed image approach to be able to experiment with benefit.

The following poem meant a lot to the boy who wrote it:

SEARCH

I hunt for meaning in a world of platitudes;
I look for truth among so many lies;
I long for love, and there is none;
I search for God, but he is gone.
But, No! I was not made in tragic mould;
So I will smile, and talk about the weather.

(S.B., Repton, England.)

This boy was also expressing a feeling which was real to him:

PRIVACY

There is so much glass in this concrete city;
What can I call my own?
Everybody sees everything which is mine;
I wish I had one corner to myself.

(T.G., Lower Canada College, Montreal, Canada.)

FORMAL PATTERNS

The pupil should be introduced at this stage to the standard metrical patterns of poetry. They have purposely been withheld until now so as to avoid establishing inflexible rhythmical stereotypes in the mind of the beginner. I have tried the alternative—that of starting complete novices on forms that must rhyme and scan—but the results have not been encouraging. The beginner frequently finds that the technicalities are too much for him and whatever interest he may have developed is thus killed before it has begun to grow.

Nevertheless, rhythm is an element common to all poetry, and young people enjoy pieces that have a distinctive sound movement, much as they appreciate music that has a pronounced beat. Practically all children hear and learn nursery rhymes when they are very young, so they are somewhat conditioned to poetry that has metrical pattern. Herein lies a danger, however. The beginner who has to write to a set rhythm must think more of words that will fit his pattern than of their appropriateness for the context. Hence his expression may become artificial. If he has been through the stages of the programme which lead to the present one, however, he should be prepared to enjoy, and derive benefit from,

working with set patterns. In fact, the discipline of having to conform to a pattern has a positive remedial effect for one whose
expression may have grown diffuse through lack of precision or
attention to detail.

Before starting the actual writing in this section, the teacher
should give a brief explanation of the rules of scansion, metre and
rhyme, placing emphasis on commonly used devices such as the
iambic foot, and the tetrameter and pentameter. Considerations of
subject matter should remain secondary here. The primary con-
cern of the pupil when attempting the proposed models should be
for a precise imitation of metre and rhyme.

RHYMED COUPLETS: These should be used as an introduction to
rhythm, and may be written in any metrical variation. The teacher
should scan a number of examples on the board, explaining them
in detail. Beginners may find it helpful to put down their ideas
in prose first. The subject they choose should be interesting and
imaginative if possible, but above all, it must be expressed with
technical accuracy.

The danger of using this device is that it may give rise to
artificial pieces such as this one:

> A bell is in the tree below,
> Its chime is like a faint bellow.

If the teacher is careful in his introduction, however, original
examples should result:

> The rocket shoots into the sky,
> A giant sparkler lofted high.
>> (P.S., Horace Mann School, New York, U.S.A.)

> The grey clouds rumble overhead,
> I listen to them warm in bed.
>> (C.R., Geelong Grammar School, Australia.)

QUATRAIN: This four-line form should be attempted with some
simple, workable pattern such as the iambic tetrameter. A lively
model should be given and the pupil asked to produce a quatrain
of his own with similar scansion. Several pauses should be made
during the actual session when lines are read out and checked so
as to help less able writers to achieve precision. A number of
variations of metre and rhyme scheme should be attempted.

This boy, in finishing a poem of four quatrains, produced the following verses:

IN A CHEAP HOTEL

Just now I crawl into my bed,
The sheets so sticky on my head;
The dripping of the bathroom tap,
It echoes like a thunder-clap.

Across the street goes off and on
And off and on and off and on
Its flashing branded on my brain—
A neon sign for Toby's Grain.

(P.C., Illawarra Grammar School, Wollongong, Australia.)

BALLAD: At this stage, the teacher should ask his pupils to do some writing of ballads. While the major emphasis must remain on precision of metre, attention should also be given to subject matter. Young people are captivated by action and adventure. The teacher should capitalize on this interest by presenting examples containing these elements in addition to some distinctive refrain. He should give a warning, however, against excessive length, exaggeration, and trite expression. The young writer may tend to get carried away by the excitement of his own narrative unless he exercises restraint.

This Australian boy wrote of the battle between a kangaroo and an evil dingo, a battle which ended on a parching plain with victory for the forces of good:

A BALLAD OF THE KANGAROO

The atmosphere is tense and still,
And from the ridges of the hill,
The plain we see, all parched and dry,
Reflecting stillness from the sky.

From tree to tree, with flitting leap,
From heat to heat, it cannot creep,
A shadow passes, quick and tense.
With buzzards staring from the fence.

A creature leaps toward the sand—
An evil dingo jumps to stand
And face his justice; great and tall,
The kangaroo brings help for all.

The kill is quick, and all rejoice,
For while you listen to my voice,
The plain is now all parched and dry,
Reflecting stillness from the sky.

(R.C., Geelong Grammar School, Australia.)

PARODY: While continuing to make accuracy of scansion the major aim, the teacher should here introduce the parody. Pupils will enjoy attempting humorous writing, and providing that they use restraint, should achieve satisfying results. I have found that enthusiasm is generated by introducing the Elizabethan lyrics "The Passionate Shepherd to His Love" by Christopher Marlowe, and "The Nymph's Reply" by Sir Walter Raleigh. I read these to the pupils and we agree that by the standards of today they reek a little too strongly of honeysuckle and violets. Nonetheless, they provide a framework within which every pupil in the class can write a plea to his own love, a parody of the original which makes contemporary appeals, and uses modern language. The plea must conform to the structure of the model and be written in quatrains containing rhymed couplets and lines of iambic tetrameter. After each pupil has written his plea—and I generally give them time to develop it at home—he should exchange it with another pupil, and they then write replies to each other after the manner of Sir Walter Raleigh.

The following two parodies gave amusement to their authors—both boys—and entertainment to their classmates:

THE TEEN TO HIS QUEEN

Come fly with me and be my girl,
And on the dance floor we will twirl
To swinging hits by Rolling Stones
Which I will buy with Daddy's loans.

We won't get home before the dawn
Although the party's on our lawn;

We'll swing and dance into the night,
And only stop when it gets light.

We'll take a trip to places far;
I'll drive you in a rented car;
But if we see funds getting low
I'll give a yell for Daddy's dough.

The way it's going things are great
It looks as though I'll be your mate;
And then when I have married you
Our kids will call me Daddy too.

(I.S., Lower Canada College, Montreal, Canada.)

The reply to the above plea was written by another boy in the same class:

THE BRUSH TO THE LUSH
I hate to say, but Daddy-o
I think you know where you can go;
Our party was a hit alright
But surely not one every night.

Although your dad gives all the gold
I don't think that our fling will hold;
I just can't stand a lazy guy
No matter how he makes me sigh.

Besides, those dances give me aches
And pains and usually it takes
About a week for them to heal
So why don't you start being real!

So to conclude I wish to say
I think you'd best be on your way;
Go find some other simpler girl
Whom round your finger you can twirl.

(J.I., Lower Canada College, Montreal, Canada.)

THE SONNET: This form gives the pupil a precise framework for his expression as it must be composed of fourteen lines, each one an iambic pentameter. The Italian sonnet develops a central idea in the octave which has an abbaabba rhyme scheme: it then presents a conclusion in the sestet which has a variable rhyme scheme. The English sonnet on the other hand, is composed of three quatrains, each having an alternating rhyme scheme, and developing a different aspect of the subject: it concludes with a unifying couplet. The teacher should introduce his pupils to both these types of sonnets, giving them some examples of precise construction such as Shakespeare's Sonnet 73.[2]

Pupils should enjoy working with this form which helps them to produce satisfying results such as the following:

SONNET TO THE MUSE EUTERPE, IN PRAISE OF MUSIC
>Euterpe, thou hast given to mankind
>The most expressive form of all the arts;
>No words can I, a humble poet, find
>To glorify the solace of men's hearts.
>But "music" now means many diff'rent things—
>Not all of them to ev'ryone appeal;
>'Tis ecstasy to some when Gigli sings,
>Though others their disgust can ill conceal.
>These ones who do not care for tenor graces
>Enjoy their music more as "folk" or "beat";
>While they show naught but pleasure on their faces,
>The classic lover's horror is complete.
>But Muse Euterpe, thou needst have no fears
>While one's own voice is music to one's ears.

>(O.P., Sydney Grammar School, Sydney, Australia.)

FURTHER FORMS: As the pupil reads and experiences more poetry, he should be encouraged to attempt imitations of the Spenserian stanza, epic, ode, and other advanced forms. The teacher should present appropriate examples from literature as models, providing detailed explanations on techniques of construction. This section should offer scope, particularly to the more able writers who should be given considerable freedom to work independently.

This piece, a modified sonnet, was written by a boy just after the death of one of his favourite poets:

ON THE DEATH OF ROBERT FROST
>Snow in your hair, sleeper.
>Snow in your hair, and love in your heart.
>Well kept the promises you left untold!
>Well worn the weary miles of snow and cold

[2] This piece is printed and discussed in Chapter 7.

Whose flakes, like silver, weave upon your head
A coronet of hope. That sleeper's bed
Was earned by glorified life unglorified,
Humanity without its taste of pride.
And what humanity—the tinkling bells,
The whining buzzes of the bushmen's knells
Were all to you a hope of life, a fount
In which the cynic's croaks might cease to count.
Let earth decide your rank? Let her proclaim
A body passed, but still a soul and name
To calm the torments of her children's mind.
And they who seek your soul; what shall they find?
Love in your heart, sleeper.
Love in your heart, and snow in your hair.

> (C.D., Lower Canada College, Montreal, Canada.)

The boy named below has written two modified Spenserian stanzas:

THE MOBILE SALESMAN

On drowsy afternoons you hear the knock
As you look up you think, the salesman—quick!
And though you'd like to bolt up key in lock,
You see a coloured thing the salesvan—slick.
It's so designed to make you want to buy;
You think you know those anti-sales adverts,
But through your reveries you hear the cry:
"Ah! Mister Smith, you have not seen our shirts!"
That happy voice—it jingles ev'ry nerve, it flirts.

You know this joker—he's been here before,
He sold you fifteen socks of different hue;
But you'll be strong, you'll say, "Get off my door!"
"Here let me show you—red and green and blue;
Or would you like a saucepan—stainless lid?
I know—some beach shoes—just the sort for you!"
He goes. You now are minus twenty quid.
Oh, who on earth could need another mop?
Oh, I've been had! Come on, let's do the mobile shop!

> (P.M., Cranbrook School, Sydney, Australia.)

PRIME-THE-PUMP INTRODUCTIONS

The three stages of this section are designed to provide the pupil with guidance in form of an increasingly flexible nature. He should by now be sufficiently familiar with techniques of structure to be capable of making choices for himself. Nonetheless, the teacher should be able to help him by providing suggestions in an introduction. The first few lines are often the most difficult for the pupil.

THE GROUP POEM: The teacher should, at least once in the year, get his class, as a group, to make a poem toward which every pupil contributes. This exercise should serve as a useful teaching device in demonstrating, particularly for the less able writers, the steps involved in building up a poem. If the exercise is to be successful, however, the teacher must do his preparation carefully, and know exactly how he wants the period to develop. Otherwise, no framework will exist for the ideas that the pupils propose, and the value of the period will be lost.

The first step in such a period is the selection of the topic. Obviously no choice can be unanimous, but it should be one that is generally agreed upon after a short discussion to which all contribute suggestions. Once the subject has been chosen—for example the Wedge-tailed Eagle—the teacher should ask what its prominent features are, and elicit such answers as eyes, wings, tail and talons. He should write these on the blackboard, and ask the pupils to suggest words which best describe each of its features. At the end of a short time the board might look something like this:

WEDGE-TAILED EAGLE

Eyes	*Wings*	*Tail*	*Talons*
evil	huge	wedge	strong
sharp	bat-like	jet-like	outstretched
menacing	spanning	wide	claw-like
watchful	silent	feathered	razor-sharp
scanning	flapping	shaped	unyielding
For what are they searching?	What are they doing? What are they like?	Of what does it remind you?	What position are they in?

He should then ask a number of questions such as the ones under the columns above. These will compel the pupils to make images, and to visualize the subject more clearly. The teacher should put down words, phrases, and statements as a progressive record of the group thinking about the subject. He should then discuss the actual structure that the poem is to have, and encourage the pupils to make a number of suggestions for it. In this way he will be leading the class through the type of selection process which every individual must go through for himself.

The class should consider such points of structure as whether the subject is best suited to a particular metrical pattern, whether the material suggests a specific concise form like the haiku, or whether a more flexible form is required. Once the structure has been established—and this should not be too difficult as all the pupils have some experience in selecting form by now—the poem should be built up line by line from the suggestions of the group. This procedure should prove rewarding for the pupils, and they will feel a sense of group accomplishment even though the poem has not come from any of them individually.

A period on the Wedge-tailed Eagle produced the following result:

WEDGE-TAILED EAGLE

Evil scanning eyes,
Searching for life below;
Bat-like wings unfold,
The king of the countryside.

Powerful wedge-tailed bird
With talons outstretched wide;
Hurtles like a thunder-bolt,
And dives on its innocent prey.

INDIVIDUAL FRAMEWORK: As an extension of the above group exercise, the teacher should present an introduction in the form of a number of leading questions. He should begin by making a general suggestion for a subject, one which he has determined after consultation with the pupils. He should ask them to write down answers to a number of questions about the topic which might be, for example, "things I like to touch". The introduction might develop somewhat in the following way:

Today I want you to think about things you like to touch. This is going to be our subject. Now I'd like you to divide the left-hand page of your exercise books into three columns, and in the middle column I want you to write down a number of the things you like to touch—put down six or seven nouns at least. Close your eyes and feel the top of your desk if you'd like. You might even imagine you are blind if that will help you. (Pause)

Now in the column to the left of the one in which you have been working, I'd like you to put any adjectives or words which tell a little more about any of the things you like to touch. To help you to do this, think about these questions: Could you say something about its colour? (Pause) Does it remind you of anything? (Pause) Can you think of an effective simile for it? (Pause) Have you given it any personality?

In the column on the right-hand side of your page write any verbs that will add meaning to the things you have mentioned. Have you really described texture? (Pause) Would someone who had never felt your object be able to get a realistic idea of it from what you have written?

Sometimes we can build up effective pictures through the use of contrasts. I want you to make on the same page, but further down in the columns, a short list of things you dislike touching. Try to choose them from your own experience. Your descriptions will be easier and more realistic if you really know what you are writing about. (Pause)

As I glance at your books, I see that you have plenty of raw material from which to make your poems. The only thing now left to decide is what form your piece is going to take. Your own material should help you to determine this. Is there a certain obvious movement suited to the words you are using? The first line is probably the most difficult one. Would any of these suggestions help you?

How I like to touch ————————— ....
Like the feel of ————————— ....
Oh! The touch of ————————— ....
The touch of ———— reminds me of ———— ....

You have about twenty-five minutes left in the period, so go ahead and work on your piece. I'm sure you'll write something you like ....

This type of introduction should not take more than ten minutes, but should help each pupil to bring to the surface ideas from which to construct his poem. The following example shows, firstly, the rough work done by a young girl:

I LIKE

bird feathers	silk	squeaks
smooth, clear	glass	spongy in my hand
foamy	rubber	it is so slippery to
slimy	mud	touch

I DON'T LIKE

scaly	fish	cold-sided
moving	ants	crawling and repulsive
sanded	balsa wood	being gnawed

From this material she constructed the poem:

THINGS I TOUCH

I love the sensation of touching slimy, slippery mud,
Or soft silk, like the feathers of a bird;
Squashed ants or cold fish make my spine tingle;
I can't bear to touch crumbling, rotting wood;
Spongy foam-rubber feels so soft on my face;
It is another thing I love to touch.

(K.M., Avalon Beach School, Sydney, Australia.)

IMAGINATIVE FIRST LINES: At this stage, the teacher should give his pupils an imaginative first line and ask them to develop it into a poem. This approach should give the young writer a start without restricting him thereafter. Metaphorically speaking, it should lead him gently toward the spout, without forcing him to drink in a particular way, or at a particular speed.

Any of the following first-line suggestions should prove useful here. They encourage the pupil to move straight into an image:

Like strings of wax, the rain fell, unending ....
Dogs, snarling, yipping, pearl-tongued ....
Siberia's sleet freezes me not ....
The moon was pasted in the sky like a wafer ....
There it lay ....

The following piece from an observant young boy illustrates this approach:

THE OLD SHOE

There it lay: a single shoe
Deserted in the gutter.
Contorted awkwardly, it had long lost its original form
And was stiffly moulded in peculiar shape.
The dusty leather bore evidence of age,
Wrinkled, like an old man's brow.
Drooping over the side was a frayed black lace;
An ant crawled about inside.

(A.G., Winchester College, England.)

OPTIC PATTERNS

The teacher may here give further freedom of structure by encouraging experimentation with form. Pupils should be asked to explore the work of contemporary writers for examples of original design. They should then do something experimental themselves, remembering that a justification should exist for the intentional shaping of any poem. I have found that many pupils get enthusiastic about optic poetry, and that they enjoy producing original shapes. I insist, however, that the content of their poems be sensible. Shape alone is not enough.

THE BOMB

I
was drinking
tea when they dropped them
and suddenly
I saw
your
face
and loved you
before the world turned upside down.

(S.B., Repton, England.)

THE PALM TREE

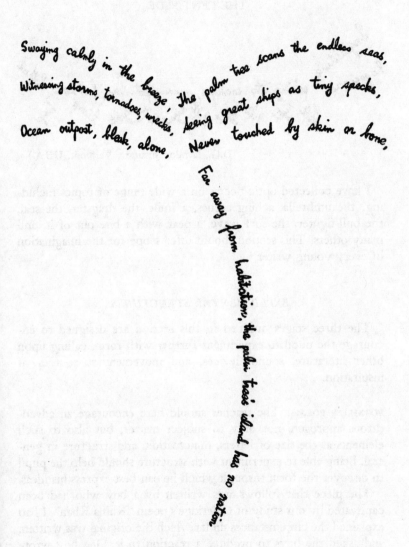

Swaying calmly in the breeze, the palm tree scans the endless seas,
Witnessing storms, tornadoes, wrecks, seeing great ships as tiny specks,
Ocean outpost, bleak, alone, Never touched by skin or bone,
For away from habitation, the palm tree's island has no nation.

(A.P., Cranbrook School, Sydney, Australia.)

Another boy achieved an unusual effect in his poem:

THE CENTIPEDE

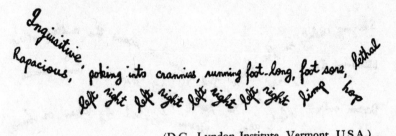

(D.G., Lyndon Institute, Vermont, U.S.A.)

I have collected optic poems on a wide range of topics including: the umbrella, aching arches, a smile, the dragster, the seal, the bull-fighter, the surf wave, a pear with a bite out of it, and many others. This section should offer scope for the imagination of every young writer.[3]

EXPERIMENTAL STRUCTURES

The three stages outlined in this section are designed to encourage the pupil to experiment further with form, calling upon other literature, sound devices, and movement as sources of inspiration.

FORMLESS POEMS: The teacher should here encourage an adventurous approach, not only to subject matter, but also to such elements as the size of letters, punctuation, and structure in general. Being able to experiment with structure should help the pupil to discover the form through which he can best express his ideas.

The piece that follows was written by a boy who had been captivated by our study of Coleridge's poem "Kubla Khan". I had explained the circumstances under which the original was written, and asked the boys to produce a reaction to it. One boy wrote this piece, and then because we were all interested, explained his thinking behind it:

[3] See Chapter 9 for further examples of optic patterns.

K.K.

Kuble Khan's pad bri...ngs out Suspense
and mystery Along with SEE mingly
MODERN LIVING his Supply of Everything does
not leave MUCH to be deSIRED the sacRED
river Alph seems to be flowing
toward cloud 7 along ETERNITY ROAD
as he flips back the pages of his Ancestral
voices for TELLING war the cOOl Abys Sinian
maid strings along on her dulcimer i was
SWING ing just as another drunk KID took
a fit and all the Milk
of Paradise.

(P.A., Lower Canada College, Montreal, Canada.)

The young writer explained that he presented "modern living" in letters of diminishing size because of his pessimism for the present generation and its future: he is optimistic toward "eternity road". "Dulcimer" he wrote on an upward slant to simulate the action of the player of the instrument, while "drunk" appears on a downward slant because wine flows in this direction. He had read some of the Freudian interpretations of Coleridge's original poem, and so wrote parts of the words "deSIRED" and "sacRED" in capital letters. He increased the size of the letters in some words such as "cOOl" in order to give them emphasis. The boy explained that he had omitted punctuation throughout the piece so as not to impede its flow.

Trying to evaluate a piece such as this is difficult by any conventional standard. Nonetheless teachers might encourage attempts like it, especially if pupils enjoy them, and think out the reasons behind their form as carefully as this boy did.

AUDIO POEMS: The pupil should be encouraged to experiment with the various sounds of poetry. In this regard, the teacher should

emphasize that the sound of a word has much to do with its interpretation, and that the sound of words in combination is an element
contributing to effective expression.

This boy made extensive use of onomatopoetic devices in his
poem:

BARBER-SHOP SYMPHONY

zzzzzz—zzz—z, click, snip-snip.
Luigi—he is my barber—
Shifts position and tilts my head.
Then zzzzzz—zzz—z, click, snip-snip.
Over there stands the soft-drink machine,
So popular in summer—
Somewhere, a radio is playing
Softly, choked by the
zzzzzz—zzz—z, click, snip-snip.
The murmurs, mumbles of other customers,
The restless rustling of magazine pages—
Luigi and the other barbers are always
Moving, shuffling feet,
From sink to chair, to sink,
To cash register.
Clickety-click, ding—
As I leave the
zzzzzz—zzz—z, click, snip-snip
Of the barber shop.

(D.C., Lower Canada College, Montreal, Canada.)

Another young writer produced this piece after we had been
studying various auditory devices for some time:

OUT OF SCHOOL

Four o'clock strikes
There's a rising hum
Then the doors fly open—
The children come.

With a wild cat-call
And a hop-scotch hop,
And bouncing a ball,
And whirling a top.

Grazing of knees
A hair pull and a slap,
A hitched-up satchel,
A pulled down cap.

Bully boys reeling off,
Hurt ones squealing off,
Aviators wheeling off
Mousy ones stealing off.

Machine-gun cries,
A kennelful of snarlings,
A hurricane of leaves,
A tree full of starlings.

Thinning away now
By some and some,
Thinning away, away,
All gone home.

(J.A., Cranbrook School, Sydney, Australia.)

If he reads, as models, pieces either from formal literature or from their own work, the teacher should be able to help his pupils to produce similar experimental audio poems for themselves.

INSIDE-OUT POEMS: This stage should be used as an extension of the section on movement already presented in Chapter Three. The teacher should encourage the pupils to exercise their imaginations in thinking of subjects which they can visualize getting inside. This exercise demands concentration, but should prove realistic for those who have already been involved in a movement sequence. The range of possible topics is extensive. The pupil should determine his form from the nature of his subject matter.

The following is one of my favourites because I recall so clearly the circumstances under which it was written. I had been asked to give a demonstration of a movement sequence for an audience of graduate students and practising teachers at the University of Sydney. Four boys from the school at which I was teaching, and who had taken part in one previous movement sequence, volunteered to be the "class" for the demonstration. Naturally they were somewhat overwhelmed when they saw all the distinguished people in the university auditorium. Just before I asked the boys onto the platform to do the sequence, I set the whole audience to writing poetry. One of the group of four boys produced the following piece:

THE UNI.

Jeepers! It's really hot in here
With all these Uni. heavies near;
I'm even writing with one's pen;
I'll never be in here again!

In a minute I'll have to get,
Up on the stage and be a jet,
Or rose, or octopus, or thumb,
Now butterflies are in my tum.

My nails are getting bitten through;
I bet you everyone will boo;
And now he's calling us to go,
I'm shivering through from head to toe.

(M.A., Cranbrook School, Sydney, Australia.)

FORM FRAMEWORK

By this stage in the programme, the pupil should be capable of determining the structure of his poems almost entirely without guidance from the teacher. He has had a range of experience in the use of different forms, and can now apply this experience to whatever material he selects.

I have found, however, that even the most able writers welcome a reminder of the various elements that their poems might contain. Hence I give them the following loosely structured framework of leading questions. These should be used as a reference only, however, and not as a rigid format. They should give each pupil some ideas as to how best to structure his material.

I have presented the questions in four general categories:

POINT OF INTEREST

What is the point of interest of your subject?
Have you established it in time, space, or mood?
Why have you chosen to write about it?
Do you want to address it, describe it, comment on it?

SENSE EXPERIENCE

What are its distinctive sensory qualities?
Does it evoke any images in your mind?
Are there some unusual characteristics about it?

EMOTIONAL RESPONSE

Is there any distinctive action, behaviour, or sensation involved?
Does it remind you of some other situation or feeling?
How do you react to it?

CONCLUSION

What awareness have you received from it?
Does it have a climax, surprise ending, or unresolved elements?
What final impression do you hope to leave?

As the number of form possibilities here is extensive, I shall give only one illustration of the type of piece that the framework can inspire:

DESTRUCTION

I watch them ripping a building down,
Demolition men near our part of town;
They can easily wreck in a day or two
What builders have taken a year to do.
And I ask myself as I go my way,
Which of these roles have I tried to play?
Am I a builder working with care,
Measuring things with a rule and square?
Or am I a wrecker who walks the town,
Content with the labour of tearing down?

(R.M., Lower Canada College, Montreal, Canada.)

COMPOSITE SEQUENCE

From this point on, the teacher should give his pupils complete freedom to choose their own forms. They should be capable of doing so. Any intrusion by the teacher on this freedom would be out of place here. However, I have found that pupils enjoy developing a single theme through a number of form stages, much as they did at the end of Chapter Two. I suggest that they try at least four different devices, and more if they wish, using the following general outline: a completed image variation, a formal pattern (such as a couplet, quatrain, or sonnet), an optic pattern, and an experimental structure, or free form. The variety of themes developed should provide pleasure for teacher and pupils alike.

The following example by an Australian boy illustrates only one of the many possibilities open at this stage:

OUTBACK

COMPLETED IMAGE

A far crack echoes, breaking the silence;
A plume of smoke shimmers in the heat;
The dust goes up my nose and wrinkles my nostrils;
The heat makes the sweat pour down.

OPTIC PATTERN

GNARLED KNOBBLY

STARVED FOR WATER

STIFLING

SURVIVING HARDLY IN THE HEAT

SILENTLY SUFFERING, NO

LAMENT

JUST

STANDING

SUFFERING

SILENTLY

FREE FORM

The goanna lies
Inert on the warm rock,
Blinking in the heat,
Staring through the shimmering veil
At the dry brown earth,
And the dusty leaves of the gum tree
Dry and scaly;
Inert on the warm rock
The goanna lies.

FORMAL PATTERN—COUPLET

The fearful desert dry and parched;
No sign of life where death's tread marched.

EXPERIMENTAL STRUCTURE

A far CRACK shatters the Silence
A DISTANT SHOT: leaves a PLUME of SMOKE —
it SHIMMERS in the SCORCHING HEAT
A BIRD flies high ENCIRCLING the prey
Then SWOOPS down
One SLASH kills the creature. The BIRD
takes 2 pecks then flies away.

(E.M., Cranbrook School, Sydney, Australia.)

G

CHAPTER 6

CONTENT CATEGORIES

The content suggestions of this chapter fall under three headings: themes from the arts, direct experiences, and triggers. As with the suggestions made in Chapter Three, those given here are intended to help the pupil in his choice of subject matter, this time at a more advanced stage in his writing.

THEMES FROM THE ARTS

SCULPTURE: As the pupils should by now be experienced in observation, they should be able to benefit both from looking at, and feeling, any piece of sculpture or carving. Recently I invited a pop-art enthusiast to show my pupils a piece which he had constructed of a coloured cube standing on its edge with a red light blinking intermittently from the top, half the toe of a shoe protruding from one of its sides, and a mouse in a treadmill against another side. The boys seemed to be able to interpret this creation, and some of them produced creditable poems as a result of it.

The teacher should encourage his pupils to study whatever piece he presents, feeling the item if they want to, and inspecting it from all angles. A connection should be suggested here with the exercises on scale from Chapter Three.

This young boy wrote the following portrait just after I had shown his class a wood-carving of a dog on the alert:

THE DOG

With the sharpest eyes and the sharpest teeth,
    The dog he guards his master;
With the sharpest nails and the sharpest ears,
    The dog he guards his master.

> Sitting, begging, chewing, eating,
> The dog he guards his master;
> Barking, howling, licking, sobbing,
> The dog he guards his master.
>
> (J.A., Cranbrook School, Sydney, Australia.)

MUSIC: If he chooses his selections with care, the teacher should find that musical stimuli are a source of inspiration to many pupils. He should capitalize on the rhythmical association between music and poetry. Since much of the earliest poetry was written to be sung to the accompaniment of stringed and wind instruments, the link between music and poetry is a natural one.

I generally use musical stimuli for five or six consecutive sessions, trying to present selections in a sequence progressing from the classical through the contemporary and eventually to electronic sounds. The pupil thus moves from greater musical structure toward less as he becomes more familiar with sound patterns.

I have found that pupils produce their most satisfactory poems when musical extracts are short—probably of less than a minute in length—and have a single theme, the aim being to avoid evoking mixed images. Experimentation should soon reveal the most successful selections for use in this way. Each teacher should develop his own list, but the following pieces should be suitable as a start:

> Wagner's Tannhäuser Overture to suggest excitement and movement;
> Saint-Saens' Organ Symphony to suggest scenes from nature;
> Beethoven's Sixth Symphony to suggest storm and strife;
> Borodin's Second Symphony to suggest peaceful situations.

The excerpt used for each creative session should be replayed a number of times while the pupils are writing. This will enable them to get the feel of the music, and even write their poems in a similar tempo if they wish. At the end of every session they should be given a chance to read their pieces to the same accompaniment. It is surprising how often expression blends effectively with the music. I try to preserve the best pieces by making a tape recording of the pupil reading his own poem with the musical extract playing in the background. I am then able to use the tape as an introduction to a later session.

The following piece was written by a young boy as he listened to the slow movement of Borodin's Second Symphony. He grasped the tone of the music, and found enjoyment in interpreting it:

TWILIGHT ON THE MARSH

Deep colours on a silent canvas,
Rich reflection in the twilight marsh,
Majestic motion through an amber dusk,
She floats—the graceful swan.

(M.R., Repton, England.)

Most pupils will find musical stimuli helpful in determining their material. The teacher should warn them, however, against directionless expression. Work produced to a musical background may wander unless the writer exercises discipline, particularly through his choice of form.

DRAMA: Through the methods advocated in this section the teacher should be able to provide an outlet for the natural interest in acting which almost every pupil has, but which he is frequently unable to release during the school day. The teacher should take every opportunity to let his pupils present their thoughts through productive channels. When he can do so in two ways at once—through both drama and written expression—a double benefit should result.

After some discussion of dramatic techniques, groups of pupils within any class should be asked to write their own short plays. I encourage them to work hard on these presentations: on the actual writing of them with a clear and definite aim; on the rehearsal, which is the key to good performance; and on the staging itself, which should be done in class as realistically as the situation permits.

The performance of the short play should occupy between five and ten minutes at the start of the lesson, after which the members of the audience should write a response in poetry to what they have just seen. The actors should write their pieces from the point of view of the characters, from the inside out so to speak.

The following poem was done by a boy just after he had watched a play on prejudice presented by his classmates:

INTOLERANCE

"Filthy Wog",
"Grasping Jew",
Do they really mean it?
How can people say these things
If they do not feel them?

Criticism,
Prejudice,
Is there nothing more?
Where has all the love gone?
Or was it never there?

Why are men so shallow?
Bitterness and
Hate.
Where will it all lead us?
Isn't it too late?

(A.R., Repton, England.)

DIRECT EXPERIENCES

A characteristic of effective writing is its realism. The teacher can help his pupils to write more realistically by enabling them to come into direct contact with live stimuli. By exposing young writers to actual situations, the teacher will be preparing them to express themselves with accuracy. The suggestions in this section are divided into three categories: research into the topic; situation outlines; and visits to places of interest.

RESEARCH INTO THE TOPIC: Ours is an age of market research. Seldom is a project started or a new item produced until a survey has been carried out. So it should be with pupils and their writing. The teacher should propose a topic for the next session, and ask them to do research on it, bringing evidence of their findings to class. Situations such as the following should prove suitable for this approach: the crowd at a sports event, as watched from a seat in the stands; the sky at night, as seen from a quiet neighbourhood park; autumn colours in the woods, as observed on a weekend walk; or a blizzard in mid-winter as experienced on the way home.

The teacher should lead a five to ten minute discussion at the start of the writing session, attempting to bring into focus the important aspects of the topic. For example, if the pupils have been investigating the sky at night, the following questions might be discussed: Precisely what colour is the sky at night? Is it darker at the centre than on the horizon? Does the moon cast shadows? What feeling do you have when you are alone under the sky?

After considering these questions, the pupils should find that they have more to say on their topic. As they have done the research, they should not be forced to invent details or to resort to clichés and trite phrases.

This young boy wrote his piece after such a discussion:

THE SKY AT NIGHT

The sky reminds me of a dark blue wash on an
      endless canvas;
Mysterious silhouettes of trees jut out against it;
Stars pave the way for the gleaming moon;
I can't understand the sky at night.

              (P.M., Canberra Grammar School, Australia.)

As a later extension of the above approach, the pupil should be asked to do some research centred more on his emotional responses than on his sensory perceptions. Experiences such as the following should prove suitable; waiting in the dentist's office; going into class on the first day of a new school year; trying to avoid an angry wasp.

In this haiku, a country boy described his after-thoughts about the last subject:

WASP

A buzzing stinger,
A bad-tempered piece of work,
A thing to beward.

              (G.S., Friends' School, Hobart, Australia.)

SITUATION OUTLINE: In this section, the teacher should try to increase realism by outlining the details of a number of specific situations. The pupils should listen to these, imagine what they are like, and then write on them in any way they wish. The teacher should build up a list of these situations, asking pupils to bring their own suggestions to add to it.

Two categories of stimuli might be used: those appealing principally to sensory description, and those appealing to emotional reaction. In the first category, any of the following should be helpful to the pupil:

Event: You are swimming underwater looking at rocks, seaweed and various shells; suddenly a large, colourful fish swims by.

Situation: Platform of a railway station late on a moonless night; a train stops and one muffled traveller gets off.

Character: weather-beaten tramp with a pack on his back, pipe, beard, and shabby clothes; he sits in a ditch by the road.

Scene: Lighthouse on a cliff projecting out to sea; water growing choppy, wind rising, and clouds scudding across the sky as a storm approaches.

The following poem was written in response to the first of the situations above:

UNDERWATER

Dive under the ocean,
Down through the slippery weeds and pale blue mist,
To a shimmering rock pool
Where the seaweed collides in the current;
Swim toward a graceful rainbow fish;
See how it races away through the mist;
Watch a colourful shell creep over the rocks;
Always look out, down here, for sharks and
    the ugly octopus.
            (P.C., Avalon Beach School, Sydney, Australia.)

In the second category, that of emotional reaction, any of the following situations should prove helpful to the young writer:

Fear: You are lying alone in your tent on a dark night, trying to fall asleep; an owl hoots, and branches creak.

Excitement: You have just arrived at a friend's house on a snowy winter morning after a long trip by sleigh through the woods; the sun is shining, and you are to spend Christmas with your friend.

Suspense: You are at the circus watching a tight-rope walker
          crossing a wire with no net below; he is caught in the
          middle, and seems about to fall.

VISITS TO PLACES OF INTEREST: As a further means of presenting
realistic stimuli to his pupils, the teacher should arrange for occa-
sional excursions outside the class. He might start by visiting the
school grounds where a range of subjects await the observer,
from garbage cans to rose bushes, from oily puddles to goal posts.
If the pupils understand that any subject that catches their attention is potential material for a poem—and the teacher should
emphasize this point by reading several effective poems on subjects not traditionally regarded as poetic—then they should readily
find sources of inspiration. Young people frequently see their
subjects from a novel point of view:

SUNFLOWER BUD

Wet and blooming bud,
Staring at the muddy ground;
The poor thing looks dead.
    (M.C., The Dragon School,
        Oxford, England.)

BELL ROPE

A long piece of rope,
Hanging from the huge steel bell,
Waiting to be pulled.
    (M.R., Geelong Grammar School,
        Australia.)

I try to take my classes outside the classroom about once a
month, sometimes to such locations as a construction site, an air-
port, a subway, a printing-press, a museum, or a zoo. Before going
on such a visit, I try to provide preparation by suggesting what
to look for on location. Unless this preparation takes place, then
the visit may be an enjoyable excursion, but will offer the pupil
little in the way of writing benefit.

TRIGGERS

This final section introduces the trigger, a term used to refer to
any stimulus presented live in the classroom to provide the pupil
with an evocative content suggestion. The teacher should plan to
introduce any trigger during the first few minutes of the period,
and let the pupils write about it for most of the rest of the session.

I have found that triggers achieve most effect if they are presented in a sequence which moves from rigid design in the early
stages toward less rigid design as the experience of the pupil

increases. By rigid design I refer to any combination of stimuli all pointing strongly towards a definite interpretation, such as pictures of a South Sea island coupled with recorded Hawaiian guitar music and the scent of perfume in the air. There is no ambiguity here, as the several sense stimuli all suggest the same theme. The teacher should be aware, however, of a potential danger. The able young writer who is using his imagination actively may find that a trigger of rigid design imposes too much of a shackle. Probably all he needs to be given is the theme, "a tropical island". Anything further in the way of audio-visual extras he may view as a restriction on his own freedom of expression. Hence I suggest that triggers move quickly in sequence towards less rigid design, where a single high-intensity suggestion without obvious interpretation is presented, such as an unanswered knocking on the door, or the ticking of a clock.

With this sequence in mind, the teacher might be ready to try some of the following suggestions before developing his own. They should be introduced live as described.

Appreciation of nature: The theme of the sea is suggested; slides of sailing ships in storms are projected on the board; selected short readings are given about the sea; a recording of storm music plays in the background.

Tragedy: Picture on the blackboard of a scene of destruction; recorded train wreck sounds; siren; reading of accident statistics.

Happiness: Picture on board of smiling young child wearing a party hat; cake on the desk with lighted candles; singing of "Happy Birthday".

Sympathy: Posters on board of children with begging bowls; display of crutches and bandages on desk; sound of crying in the background.

Surprise: Pile of blankets in front of the class; suddenly a pupil leaps from them with a scream, and runs out of the room; or, janitor with pail and mop climbs the fire escape; enters the class noisily by the emergency window; and walks through, whistling.

Mystery: Gun lying on the desk, and sign over it reading, Firearms, do not touch; or, urgent unanswered rapping at the door; or, the recorded last moments of a rocket firing count-down.

After the teacher has presented several triggers himself, he should turn the responsibility over to his pupils. I vividly recall coming to class one day and having the boy in charge of the period tell us to put our heads on our desks, and close our eyes. As soon as we did this, he pulled down the blinds so that the room was in almost total darkness. He then hung over the light above the blackboard a thick piece of hangman's rope, at the end of which was a large noose. As the light shone on it, the rope stood out stark against the dark background. The boy then switched on a portable tape machine on which he had recorded twenty minutes of a grandfather clock ticking—loudly. He then told us to open our eyes.

The effect created in the dark room was startling. Some of the boys were writing almost immediately. Others sat for fifteen minutes before beginning. Nearly everyone produced something which, by his own standard, was unusual. The following piece by a fourteen-year-old boy, who two nights earlier had seen a television documentary on a German prison camp, illustrates the impact of this trigger:

AUSCHWITZ

The ruthless, incessant sound of a death march
    resounds, heartless.
How many have preceded this one?
How terrible is the rope of death.
This is no ordinary execution.
The S.S. have made *you* pull the death wagon.
It has a rickety wheel.
You must lead a fellow man to death.
This is no ordinary execution;
Your brother is going to die.

It is a long march through Auschwitz;
The eyes of prisoners bulge with hate of the Nazi,
As they see the head of the condemned
    hung low over his chest.

They wish they did not have to watch.
The rope swings overhead.
They will not let you speak to say
    goodbye to your own brother.
How can you exchange love and farewell
    in a last glance?
It is so heartless;
Your brother swings, limp.
Don't break up! You can't! You mustn't!
It is a *normal* day at Auschwitz.

(W.D., Lower Canada College, Montreal, Canada.)

I have since used this trigger many times myself with similar results. As with most triggers that are carefully presented, it seems to unify a number of forces under the kind of tension which enables pupils to produce effective writing.

CHAPTER 7

EVALUATION EXERCISES

Pupils should have had sufficient writing experience by this stage of the programme to benefit from more advanced exercises in evaluation. The teacher should refer to the work of practising writers in helping his pupils with any difficulties they are facing. Improved expression usually comes with a greater knowledge of techniques. This chapter puts forward suggestions for introducing young writers to ideas that may be new to them, and is divided into three main sections: assessment of poetry; the craftsmanship of the poet; and outside-class projects.

ASSESSMENT OF POETRY

The pupil should begin any assessment by determining whether or not the poem meets the technical requirements of its form. For example, if the poem is a haiku, does it have three lines of five, seven and five syllables respectively? Or if it is a sonnet, does it contain fourteen lines, each an iambic pentameter? After the technical correctness of the poem has been established, the pupil should apply the questions of the framework to it,[1] placing emphasis on sincerity, and originality of approach. Perhaps only the writer himself can truly assess sincerity. Nonetheless, any genuine piece should ring true even to the reader who has not actually experienced the situation described in the poem.

TECHNIQUES OF UNDERSTANDING: The pupil will get more enjoyment from a poem if he knows how to extract meaning from it; or, speaking metaphorically, if he knows how to squeeze the

[1] The framework for evaluation is detailed in Chapter 4.

orange so as to get every drop of juice from it. This process will involve a number of readings, and a knowledge of techniques.

I try to illustrate these techniques by applying them to one of a number of suitable poems, for example, Sonnet 73 by Shakespeare. Without any formal introduction or further instructions, I present a copy of the sonnet to pupils and give them ten minutes to evaluate it. Those who are superficial in their treatment, or who are inexperienced in the skills of evaluation, get little meaning from it. I then ask the class to follow a number of planned stages with me, knowing that, at the end of them, the meaning of the poem will become clearer:

SONNET 73

That time of year thou may'st in me behold
When yellow leaves, or none, or few, do hang
Upon these boughs which shake against the cold,
Bare ruin'd choirs, where late the sweet birds sang.
In me thou see'st the twilight of such day
As after sunset fadeth in the west,
Which by and by black night doth take away,
Death's second self, that seals up all in rest.
In me thou seest the glowing of such fire
That on the ashes of his youth doth lie,
As the death-bed whereon it must expire,
Consum'd with that which it was nourish'd by.
    This thou perceiv'st which makes thy love more strong,
    To love that well which thou must leave ere long.

We discuss the theme of the sonnet. After a short time the class agree that it is about growing older and the implications that this has both for the writer, who is the speaker in the piece, and the reader, who is the listener. One of the keys to unlocking the meaning of this poem is for the pupil to recognize that it is an English sonnet, and as such is composed of three quatrains and a couplet. Each of the quatrains develops a different aspect of the subject, and the couplet unifies these aspects at the end. Rather than attack the sonnet as a whole, the pupil should first consider each of its quatrains individually.

A careful reading will show him that the theme of the first quatrain is a season of the year, autumn; that the theme of the second quatrain is a time of day, twilight; and that the theme of the third quatrain is a focal point of interest, a dying fire. He should thus understand that Shakespeare is presenting his images in ascending order of importance, beginning with an entire season, and concentrating finally on a particular object, at a specific time, on a single day. This is the same technique the camera-man uses when he moves from a wide-lens picture of a scene into a close-up of the point of interest.

This, however, is only the first stage involved in getting the full meaning from the sonnet. The pupil should now reread it more slowly, and discover how each quatrain is constructed. He should observe that in building up his picture of autumn, Shakespeare makes use of other sub-images, namely trees, leaves, and silent choirs. Likewise in writing about twilight, Shakespeare refers to a fading sunset, black night, and sleep. He comes to the climax of his images in the quatrain on the dying fire where he speaks of glowing embers, ashes, and the death-bed of youth.

A further reading should reveal the significance of each individual line in each quatrain, and its contribution to the meaning of the sonnet as a whole. At this stage, the pupil should be able to appreciate the appropriateness of one of the finest lines in English poetry:

"Bare ruin'd choirs, where late the sweet birds sang."

Every word is precise in its selection, and combines with every other word to produce the exact image.

After the pupil has finished his study of the three quatrains, he should read the final couplet, which draws the whole sonnet together giving significance to each of its parts.

Once the teacher has been able to guide his pupils through the stages outlined above, he should have no difficulty in convincing them that enjoyment and meaning come from intensive reading, and that without this, little value is discovered in any poem. Such an illustration of the techniques involved in understanding any piece should enable the pupils to carry out their own similar studies on other poems they read.

COMPARISON OF POEMS: As an extension of the section on constructive criticism from Chapter Four, and as a sequel to the exercise suggested above, the teacher should ask his pupils to make a comparison of a number of pairs of poems. For this purpose, they should use the criteria with which they are already familiar.

The teacher should introduce a number of pairs of poems by recognized writers, as well as by his own pupils. In the early stages particularly, the poems taken as examples should differ sufficiently to present a contrast to even the least able pupils.

This exercise should not be misused, however. I recall seeing in a pupil's work book some time ago two pieces of writing with the following introduction:

Compare the two passages below and ask yourself these questions:

> Which is the more worthwhile in content?
> Which contains more skilful word associations?
> Which has the greater claim to be called poetic?

(i)

I like pudding
Pudding for me!

I like it for dinner,
I like it for tea,
A little each day
Is a fine recipe.

I like pudding,
Pudding for me!

(ii)

Blessed are the poor in spirit, for theirs is the kingdom
    of heaven;
Blessed are they that mourn, for they shall be comforted;
Blessed are the meek, for they shall inherit the earth.

Asking pupils to make comparisons between two such pieces as these is, to me, misleading, and defeats the purpose of the exercise. Pupils should not be given the suggestion that pudding is an unworthy topic on which to write, or indeed that every Biblical passage is necessarily of literary merit.

Two poems such as the following, however, both on the theme of death, should offer the pupil a more worthwhile task:

(i)

Buffalo Bill's
   defunct
           who used to
                  ride a watersmooth-silver
                                    stallion
   and break onetwothreefourfive pigeonsjustlikethat
                                    Jesus
      he was a handsome man
                  and what i want to know is
      how do you like your blueeyed boy
      Mister Death.

(ii)

   It seemed your childish feet were tired of straying;
   You did not greet me from your flower-strewn bed;
   Yet still I knew that you were only playing,
   Playing at being dead.

The pupils should be able to recognize that, despite its lack of
superficial polish, the first poem expresses an emotional sincerity
which is in sharp contrast to the artificial sentimentality of the
second. The training involved in making such distinctions should
help them to improve their own writing.

THE CRAFTSMANSHIP OF THE POET

The teacher should constantly be seeking ways to bring home
to his pupils the point that while writing is enjoyable, it also
demands concentration and care. Like Edison's view of genius,
effective expression is ninety-nine per cent perspiration, and one
per cent inspiration. I have found that a useful way of emphasizing this point is to introduce pupils to the work of established
poets. Stephen Spender in his book *The Making of a Poem*,
stresses the importance of rewriting and polishing original expression. Of value is his description of how he achieved a particular effect in one of his poems:

   In the next twenty versions of the poem I felt my way
   towards the clarification of the seen picture, the music and
   the inner feeling. In the first version . . . . there is the phrase in
   the second and third lines

(a)   The waves
Like wires burn with the sun's copper glow,

This phrase fuses the image of the sea with the idea of music, and is therefore a key-phrase because the theme of the poem is the fusion of the land with the sea. Here then are several versions of these one and a quarter lines, in the order in which they were written:

(b)   The waves are wires
Burning as with the secret song of fires

(c)   The day burns in the trembling wires
With a vast music golden in the eyes

(d)   The day glows on its trembling wires
Singing a golden music in the eyes

(e)   The day glows on its burning wires
Like waves of music golden to the eyes

(f)   Afternoon burns upon its wires
Lines of music dazzling the eyes

(g)   Afternoon gilds its tingling wires
To a visual silent music of the eyes

In the final version, these two lines appear as in the following stanza:

(h) There are some days the happy ocean lies
Like an unfingered harp, below the land.
Afternoon gilds all the silent wires
Into a burning music of the eyes.[2]

An illustration of this type should help to convince pupils that precise expression comes as a result of determination, technical knowledge, and patience on the part of the writer. Copies of this, or any other example, should be distributed to the members of the group, and used as the basis for class discussion.

The teacher should extend this section to include aspects of the craft of the poet which might prove helpful to the pupils with their own writing. This exercise should reinforce the principle of learning through doing, and provide another link between this programme and the formal study of poetry in the English course.

[2] Spender, S., *The Making of a Poem*. London, Hamish Hamilton, 1955, pp. 51-2.

OUTSIDE-CLASS PROJECTS

Several times in every year—perhaps at the end of each term—
the teacher may give his pupils a major outside-class project. This
project should serve as a review of a block of work just completed, in addition to giving the pupils a chance to break new
ground through reading and independent research. The teacher
should plan his assignments to coincide with various sections of
the programme, and should give his pupils ample time to complete
them.

In the early stages, I frequently set an assignment which requires
some research into the processes involved in the act of creation.
Pupils are asked to investigate such stages as preparation, incuba-
tion, illumination, and verification. Having done so, they should
be better prepared to understand what is taking place every time
they try to write themselves, and why the creative process is
frequently a slow and sometimes a frustrating one.

At a later stage I asked the pupils to produce a poem on any
subject, and in any form of their choice. After writing the poem,
each pupil must give a prose explanation of such points as why
he selected his subject, how he tried to develop it, and what degree
of success he felt he achieved.

The example cited below from a fourteen-year-old writer illustrates the possible results of such a project. It reveals a conscious
attention to details which might not have been given were it not
for the assignment.

OVERBREED

Through a stifling haze of depression
Are seen multitudes of grey, stick-like people,
Living in a landscape of their own creation—
A world covered in splotches of white, yellow, brown, and black,
Cemented together by brick and stone, steel and concrete,
Choking out the simplest roots of spirit.

(R.D., Lower Canada College, Montreal, Canada.)

The pupil commented on his work in part as follows:

I first looked for a topic on which to write. This subject was
influenced by my emotions at the time. If I had written the poem
at intervals, its mood would have changed at each interval, and
the essential spirit I was trying to convey would thus have been

lost. I believe that in any poem a vital essential is to express spirit, individual spirit; this spirit is the goal of what is created. . . .

Just before writing the poem, I had arrived home after taking a ride on a particularly dirty bus through a depressing part of the city. The day was overcast and sombre. I certainly have no liking for metropolitan buses, as I must use them every school day of the year. They are such drab vehicles. It seemed to me that the architects who built the homes in this area had tried to make each one as conformist as the next. The same red-bricked rows gave the district an unpleasant atmosphere of uniformity. There was nothing distinctive about any of the houses, and this is something from which I recoil. The setting was altogether too machine-like for me. It had the *1984* feeling. I linked this mood with a topic I had read about a few days earlier in an article by Sir Julian Huxley on man's greatest problem—over-breeding. The fusion of these two elements—mood and topic—provided the inspiration for my poem.

The teacher should develop his own projects on different aspects of the programme. These should be designed to give the pupils enjoyment and profit by offering them an opportunity to investigate areas that interest them.

I have been urging throughout these chapters that teachers should develop their own approaches and additions to the suggestions which I have made. From this stage on, every teacher should seek to extend the programme in his own practice and experience, as I shall in mine.

CHAPTER 8

PRINCIPLES

Some teachers may feel that creative writing either comes naturally, or that only two or three pupils in any of their classes have been born with the ability for it, and that there is therefore little point in trying to help the majority of the class to achieve it. My experience has been that, given some guidance in form, content, and evaluation, almost every pupil in a group will eventually be able to produce something that satisfies him. The task facing the teacher is to provide such guidance in a firm yet unobtrusive way, at the same time building the confidence of the beginner.

This chapter is made up of eight sections containing principles with which every teacher should be familiar.

I suggest that the programme should be started on the basis of one period per week in the first year of secondary school—although it can be used with equal impact in the primary school—and maintained throughout subsequent years on a similar basis, or even extended to two periods per week where the timetable permits. Teachers who are able to give some of their prose-composition time to this programme may be surprised at the interest it generates and the results it helps the pupils to produce.

THE CREATIVE CLIMATE

1. ATMOSPHERE: Every teacher is faced with the task of developing, in his own classroom, a suitable climate for creative work. He must convince his pupils—largely by his own attitude and example—that the writing of poetry can be a rewarding enterprise. He should stress that poetry imposes no restrictions of subject matter or structure, and that its range is as extensive as the imagination of the writer.

2. TRANSFER: This programme is designed for use as part of the formal English course, and frequently in place of—or at least in conjunction with—work in prose composition. The pupil should find his practical writing experience of value in his appreciation of the work of established poets. It is surprising how his respect for the work of the masters increases after he has attempted to write on similar subjects himself. In order to have a record of his progress, each pupil should keep a special exercise book for his creative writing.

3. PARTICIPATION: Every teacher of English should be a practising writer himself, regardless of his standard. It is only through trying the various forms that he introduces to his pupils that he is able to appreciate what is involved in writing them. Pupils have added respect for the teacher who is willing, not only to assign exercises, but to attempt them himself.

FORM AND STRUCTURE

1. SEQUENCE OF STAGES: The beginner welcomes advice as to how to shape his expression. He may have some imaginative material in mind, but is likely to be uncertain about what structure it should take. Hence he should be introduced to a number of specific forms.

These should be presented in a sequence which moves from relative rigidity at the start, toward greater freedom as he develops familiarity with different approaches, and is more capable of making selections for himself. Giving the pupil complete freedom of form at the beginning usually turns him to random structural experimentation, which seldom produces the rewards associated with controlled expression.

2. ACHIEVABLE STEPS: The forms presented should be achievable by all, including the slower pupils, within the allotted writing time. The teacher should introduce new stages at a pace in keeping with the interest and rate of progress of each particular group. If a phase is generating excitement, it should be extended for further periods. Every teacher should try to develop a sensitivity to the feelings of his groups, and hence adapt his programme accordingly.

3. POTENTIAL DANGER: Within any class there may be a handful of pupils who are already writing poetry on their own. Adherence

to set forms may appear a restriction to them because they are used to letting their material establish its own structure. They should be encouraged to follow the programme with the others, however, thus broadening their own experience with different approaches. An aim of the programme is ultimately to enable every pupil to choose his own form without any guidance from the teacher.

CHOICE OF MATERIAL

1. GUIDANCE: Most pupils, including the so-called unimaginative ones, should have little difficulty in providing themselves with subjects on which to write, especially if they have been encouraged to explore their surroundings, and follow up their own interests. As the programme progresses, however, some content suggestions from the teacher should be useful, principally to add variety and scope to the whole approach.

2. SINCERITY: Pupils should realize that genuineness of expression is an important mark of quality in any writing. As one boy put it: "It doesn't much matter what you write about, so long as you're sincere." Sincerity will more readily be attained if the pupil knows that he may write about any subject that interests him. He can often get inspiration from the most unlikely—and seemingly unpoetic—sources if his attention is turned to them:

THE PLACE OVER THE FENCE

The sludge is getting worse by the day;
That slimy pipe is obstructed again;
Drainwater trickles around a hairless dead cat;
Thick yellow froth infests a long-abandoned chunk of bread.
(R.D., Cranbrook School, Sydney, Australia.)

Perhaps this element of sincerity is what most truly gives value to any creative work. It is the heart, without which any piece is but a hollow shell.

3. IMAGINATION: I am always disappointed when a pupil says to me, "But I have no imagination." This statement suggests one of two things: either he has been told this by an adult, or he has not been trained to make use of the antennae which we all have, such as eyes, and ears. Everyone has imagination. It is not, however, a

static faculty, but like many others, one which requires regular exercise. Part of the responsibility of the teacher is to lead his pupils toward a heightened sensitivity to things around him, and hence toward the increased ability to respond to them imaginatively.

PREPARATION FOR WRITING

1. READINESS: Before the pupil is asked to write, he should receive some preparation for his task. This preparation might take a number of forms, two of which follow. Firstly, he should do the exercises provided in Chapter Two to help him become more conscious of words and their uses. Secondly, he should be trained to sharpen his powers of observation so that he may become increasingly aware of senses and emotions.

2. RECORDING EXPERIENCES: As an extension of the above principle, each pupil should keep a notebook in which he should record the outline of any experience that appears memorable. This notebook will serve as a source of subject material for actual classroom writing sessions. A number of poets, among them Robert Graves and Stephen Spender, use this technique. Consciously attempting to capture the moment is an effective way of extending one's powers of observation.

3. LIVE STIMULI: The teacher should, wherever possible, enable his pupils to have some direct contact with their subjects before they are set to writing about them. This contact might take the form of a preparatory assignment. The pupils should be asked to go out into a quiet neighbourhood park and record the sights and sounds of the sky at night, returning to the next session with their material. It might equally involve a visit, during class time, to some such location as a local park, foundry, zoo, or the like. These experiences should make it easier for pupils to express themselves with accuracy.

The teacher should also make provision for observation periods at intervals. These should be conducted orally. Rupert Brooke said that it was good to read poetry, better to write poetry, and best of all to live poetry. For the pupil, being able to find joy in ordinary things is probably the best way of living poetry. He will not develop an awareness, however, unless his eyes and ears are open. In the observation period, he should be asked to tell the class about something he saw on the way to school, at the beach, in the bush, or somewhere else. The teacher should insist on detailed observations. A pupil might say, "I saw a pepper tree." This will not do. But if he can be trained to say, "I saw a tree which sparkled with sunlight. It had a spidery look about it, like a curtain of green fishbones", then it is more likely that his poem about it will be vivid.

4. ILLUSTRATION: The pupil might occasionally be asked to illustrate his subject—preferably in colour—before he begins to write about it. Being thus compelled to concentrate on such elements as colour, movement, and dimension, the pupil should be better prepared to write about them afterwards. The final product on paper of this combination of literature and art is often pleasing to the eye.

THE CLASSROOM INTRODUCTION

1. TONE: The teacher should realize that his five to ten minute introduction to the writing session will have a significant influence on the outcome of the period. For this reason, he should carry out his preparation with care, and know exactly what he is trying to achieve by each of his instructions. He needs, for example, to vary his approach so as to get through to different age groups with equal force. The classroom introduction should be as captivating as possible, yet it should appear to be unfolding in an unrehearsed, relaxed way. The teacher should thus attempt to transmit to his pupils a confidence in their ability to do the job, and an enthusiasm to get on with it.

2. POWER OF SUGGESTION: The teacher should present his introduction slowly and clearly, using the blackboard to illustrate his forms. He should answer questions patiently, making sure that every pupil understands the aim of the session. He should also realize that the examples he reads will have an influence on the choice each pupil makes for his own topic. The teacher should give illustrations which are strong without being overpowering, and which offer scope for constructive comments.[1] The pupil is

[1] A poem such as "*Porta Vacat Culpa*" on p. 28 is overpowering. If it is read as an introductory example many pupils may write on a similar topic in a similar tone. A poem such as "The Desert by Night" on p. 62 appears more suitable, however, and gives the teacher opportunity to comment on conciseness, reserve, and vivid imagery.

likely to be influenced by any suggestion from the teacher, however indirect it may appear. On a recent visit to a school I intentionally placed an apple in the middle of my pile of books on the desk, and only partially visible. I made no reference to the apple in my introduction, nor did I even glance in its direction. Yet when the poems came in—and the pupils had been given complete freedom to choose their own subjects—four out of six in the front row—unknown to each other—had written about apples. As I had previously never received a single poem about an apple (in more than fifty thousand collected), the result appeared significant.

3. TIMING: Since the moment at which the pupil picks his subject is evidently highly charged (as one pupil put it, "He's thrown me into the middle of the pool, and now I've got to swim"), the teacher's sense of timing must be acute. As the programme continues, however, and the pupil is more strongly motivated from within than from without, the elements of suggestion and timing should become less significant.

THE WRITING SESSION

1. PROCEDURE: The central unit of the programme is the individual classroom period, and virtually all writing takes place within it. A period should consist of a five to ten minute introduction by the teacher dealing with the objectives for the session; twenty-five to thirty minutes for the writing itself; and a final five to ten minutes for the reading by the pupils of the work they have produced. The writing session should occur, wherever possible, in the same period on the timetable every week so that the pupil may prepare himself for it.

2. CONCENTRATION: One of the elements vital to the success of any writing session is concentration on the part of every pupil. This involves becoming enveloped in his own thoughts, and escaping the restrictions which the four walls of the classroom present. Those who, for one reason or other, have been unable to do so, will find writing difficult. In order to give everyone a chance to become involved with his own subject, complete silence should be maintained during the actual writing. Any kind of disturbance proves upsetting and may destroy whatever feeling of

aloneness with his subject the pupil has been able to create. The establishment of this atmosphere of concentration is a matter for the very first session. The teacher should outline his expectations quite firmly, adding to his statement an explanation of the reasons behind his demands. Once this atmosphere has been established, every pupil should have a chance to produce satisfying results.

3. TENSION: Most pupils welcome the tension of the writing session, and derive benefit from the discipline that the time restriction imposes—benefit that extends even into such areas as the writing of examinations. I use the term tension to refer to the combination of elements such as time limits, space restrictions, feelings of excitement, and the like, which exist in the classroom. I have found that this tension acts positively for almost every pupil in helping him to produce something within the period. He gains encouragement from seeing others around him writing. Teachers should not confuse the term tension with the term pressure, however. The former should be a positive, helpful force. The latter is a negative one, associated with the type of thoughtless action which prompts a teacher, shortly after he has started his class on their writing, to walk around the room looking over shoulders to see whether the pupils have done anything yet. Once the introduction is complete, it is important that the teacher become as unobtrusive as possible.

4. SAFEGUARDS: One must make provision for the pupil who, though of good intention, is simply not in the mood to produce anything on a particular day. I try to play down this situation—and, in fact, it seldom occurs—but when it does, I am sympathetic and encourage the pupil to try again at home, perhaps changing his subject and approach. The teacher should not be primarily concerned with the actual results obtained from any given session. Whatever piece is produced on the spot should serve as the embryo only of an eventually completed poem, and the session itself as one in which interest is stimulated for the future. Any impatience by the teacher at a lack of on-the-spot results would be unwise. Creation simply doesn't work this way.

CONSTRUCTIVE EVALUATION

1. POSITIVE APPROACH: The term analysis is a negative one, with overtones of the destructive rather than the constructive. The

teacher should develop a positive approach to evaluation, presenting it as an exercise in seeing, admiring—even criticizing—how a poem is put together, and not as a dissection, or exercise in tearing apart. This emphasis is an important one for the pupils as they approach evaluation.

2. TECHNIQUES: The pupil needs to be shown that evaluation involves skills that must be learned and practised. Getting the meaning from a poem is rather like squeezing an orange. If you are patient, thorough, and have the "know how" you get a good deal of juice and drinking pleasure: otherwise—and if you fail to work at it—you don't.[2] Understanding is based on a knowledge of techniques, and not merely on unsubstantiated feeling. Experienced teachers realize that well-prepared pupils can discriminate between writing which is effective, and that which lacks precision. One need only read a number of poems of a set type to a class—haikus let us say—and notice how, with those which are well-expressed, a ripple of recognition runs through the class. With pieces of little merit, on the other hand, practically no response occurs.

3. TIMING: The aim of all evaluation is to heighten enjoyment by increasing understanding. It is therefore most fruitful when it arises in response to a desire by the pupil to improve his own writing. The teacher should not hurry the introduction of evaluation exercises, but rather he should wait until the pupil feels the need for it, and hence is prepared for the grammar lesson in palatable form. The teacher should also be sure that the pupil has passed the tender stage of his early writing before he offers any tougher guidance on technique. Lasting damage may be done by the teacher who, perhaps even unwittingly, is unduly critical of the first pieces a pupil produces. The trust that any young writer offers when he gives himself to his work should be regarded as an almost sacred thing.

4. MOTIVATION: The teacher should be aware of various methods for increasing interest in the writing programme. He might have class wallboards and display exemplary work; he might publish a class paper, or use the school magazine; he might establish interclass poetry exchanges, thus giving recognition to young writers

[2] See the evaluation of Sonnet 73 in Chapter 6.

by letting them read their work to other forms; he might encourage group recitation of some of the best pieces. Regardless of what he does in these superficial ways, however, it is even more important that he remain alive and sensitive himself, ready again to be filled with excitement by the work that each new group produces.

REVISION AND POLISHING

1. REWRITING: The teacher should impress his pupils with the necessity of polishing their expression. They should understand that there is nothing sacrosanct about their original wording. In fact, experienced writers realize that before the final version is achieved, much reworking of the initial piece is required. Pupils must realize that this programme promises no short-cuts to success.

2. STAGES OF REVISION: The process of revision should occur in two stages: in the initial writing period itself, and again after a lapse of time during which original expression has been allowed to grow cold. In the former stage, the left-hand page of the special exercise book should be used as a drafting-board for all writing, with alterations being made on it. Once the final version is produced to the satisfaction of the pupil, it should be recorded in pencil on the right-hand page. The pupil should also write a prose comment on each of his poems, recording it at the bottom of the right-hand page. This comment should contain the answers to a variety of questions: Where did he get his inspiration? Is he satisfied with the result? Did he try to achieve any particular effects? Having to answer these questions should make the young writer more conscious of his goals. This should complete the first stage of the polishing process. The second stage will probably not occur until several sessions later when the pupil is given a period for reviewing his previous three or four pieces, and making whatever alterations he wants. Having done the original version in pencil only, he will have less difficulty in making changes than if he had written it in ink.

3. REINFORCEMENT AFTER WRITING: Immediately after the pupil has produced his poem, and during the last five or ten minutes of the period, he should be given a chance to read his work aloud. The difficulty of finding time for every pupil to read probably

cannot be overcome; however, it should be possible to establish a satisfactory rotation system. The teacher should give less able pupils just as much chance to present their work as he gives brighter ones. He should call on them directly if they are reticent in volunteering, especially after he has seen their books, and knows that a number of them have good results. Devoting some time to reading at the end of every period seems to tie the session together, particularly if the pupils have been trained to read so as to give life to their work. The teacher should stress that poetry is written primarily to be read aloud, and that many of its beauties remain hidden unless this happens. A poem that is not heard is, in many senses, as lifeless as a record that is not played.

4. EXPECTATION: A final warning should be sounded as to the rewards that may reasonably be expected from the programme. The pupil must realize that achievement comes, not through the efforts of the teacher, but as a result of his own enthusiastic participation; while for his part, the teacher should be patient, and not expect quick results.

For teachers who are interested in following up any of the principles of this chapter, I have constructed a table of references to twenty distinguished writers in the field. I have kept this list short so that it will be workable. Across the top of this table, and in the same order in which they have already been presented, are the eight areas with which the principles deal. A ninth column, headed "specific comment", has been added for further remarks. Down the left-hand side of the table (in alphabetical order and with numbers corresponding to those of the Select Bibliography) appear the names of the twenty writers.

It is not my intention to judge the relative merits of the work of these writers. For the sake of convenience, I have used a three star system, placing one, two, or three stars in the appropriate squares on the table depending, mainly, on how much attention each author has given to the principle under consideration. I have tried to include in every assessment, however, some measure of judgment concerning the value of each piece of writing to interested readers. Where no star appears under a principle, the indication is that the author has not been concerned at all—or at least only marginally—with it.

TABLE OF REFERENCES

AUTHOR	Creative Climate	Form and Structure	Choice of Material	Preparation for Writing	Classroom Introduction	Writing Session	Constructive Evaluation	Revision and Polishing	Specific Comment
1 APPLEGATE	**	*	**	*			*	*	Original content ideas
2 BALDWIN	*	*	**	*				*	Approach for enjoyment
3 BROOKS	**	**	*	*			***	**	Evaluation strong
4 CLEGG		*	*				**	*	Pupil's examples good
5 COOPER	*	*	**				**		Evaluation of pupil's work good
6 CROSS	*	*		*			**	*	Critical questions good
7 DRUCE	**	*	***	**	*	*	***	***	I like this best
8 FORD	*	*	**	*			**	*	Good anthology
9 HOLBROOK	**	*	**				**	**	Reliable
10 HOOK	**	**	*	*	*		*	**	Useful form exercises

AUTHOR	Creative Climate	Form and Structure	Choice of Material	Preparation for Writing	Classroom Introduction	Writing Session	Constructive Evaluation	Revision and Polishing	Specific Comment
11 KNAPP	**	*	**				*	*	Practical
12 LANGDON	**	*	***	*	*	*	*	*	Pupil preparation good
13 LEWIS	*	*	*				**	*	Constructive comparisons
14 MEARNS	**		**	*	*		*	*	Enthusiastic
15 MOSBY	*	*	***			*		*	Material original
16 O'DONNELL	**	*	*				**	*	Realistic
17 REEVES	*	**	*	*			**		Analytically strong
18 ROWE	*	*	***				*	*	Subject suggestions good
19 SWEETKIND	*	**	*				**	*	Sound approach
20 WALTER	***	**	**	**		*	*	**	One of the best

NOTE. See page 133 for titles, publishers, etc., of the books by these authors.

CHAPTER *9*

A SHORT ANTHOLOGY OF POEMS

In this concluding chapter I have presented a selection of poems by young writers from different countries. The pieces are offered principally for the enjoyment of the reader, and as further illustration of the fact that pupils can write with pleasure and benefit to themselves if they are encouraged to do so. I have grouped the poems according to their forms, and included a short general section at the end.

EZRA POUND COUPLET

A city tramp searching through garbage;
A hungry crab on a holiday beach.

(M.E., Cranbrook School, Sydney, Australia.)

A speeding jet in a high-speed curve;
A hawk gliding with wings outstretched.

(D.M., Lower Canada College, Montreal, Canada.)

A man in a cell;
A fish in a bowl.

(C.W., Riverside High School, Launceston, Australia.)

A soldier firing his gun;
A chameleon shooting out its tongue.

(H.H., Belmont High School, Boston, U.S.A.)

The scratching of a pen on paper;
A cat asking to come in out of the cold.

(P.G., Bishop's College School, Lennoxville, Canada.)

A hydrofoil skimming over the sea;
A bicycle zipping through a puddle.

(R.G., Canberra Grammar School, Australia.)

A sky writer's trail zig-zagging across the heavens;
A child's careless scribbling on a page.

(B.M., Presbyterian Ladies' College, Melbourne, Australia.)

A lion in the bush roaring;
Your father in the house calling.

(J.S., Friends' School, Hobart, Australia.)

FORM POEM

CHEMISTRY MISFORTUNE

Excitement, tweezers, chemicals, door,
   Tubes, box, room,
Glass, jar, crystals, floor,
   Scoop, powder, BOOM!

(P.V., The Grange School, Santiago, Chile.)

THE HUNT

Men, horses, dogs, fox,
   Horn, gallop, yell,
Hedges, fences, streams, haycocks,
   Whining, baying, knell.

(P.R., Winchester College, England.)

MY FIRST DAY ON ICE

Slipping, sliding, skimming, smash,
    Up, down, smack,
Lookout, swerve, missed, crash,
    Brake, stop, crack.

(M.M., School 52, Moscow, U.S.S.R.)

DESTRUCTION

Old-fashioned, stately, respected, loved,
    Pillared, brass-knobbed, polished,
Rumbles, tractors, battered, shoved,
    Trembling, swaying, demolished.

(S.V., Ridley College, St. Catharine's, Canada.)

THE U.S.A.

Sweaters, jeans, bike, sin,
    Coffee-bar, juke-box, jive,
Flick-knife, pin-ups, cigarettes, gin,
    Grown-up, job, ALIVE.

(R.M., Repton, England.)

SCHOOL

School, bell, assembly, Science,
    History, Music, bore,
German, library, Maths, defiance,
    French, bottom, sore.

(L.M., Kuringai High School, Sydney, Australia.)

CHARLIE CHAPLIN

Hat, stick, pigeon toe,
    Girl, villain, train,
Untie, custard, pie, throw,
    Run, jump, insane.

(A.G., Lower Canada College, Montreal, Canada.)

FASHION PARADE

Elegant, slim, turning, smiling,
  Swaying, dashing, light,
Clapping, cheering, moving, changing,
  Backwards, forwards, bright.
    (K.B., J. J. Cahill High School, Sydney, Australia.)

MY BROTHER

Tease, cry, disturb, annoy,
  Yell, grab, row.
Scream, pinch, kick, oh-boy,
  Ready, aim, POW!
    (M.B., Sydney Grammar School, Sydney, Australia.)

PAINTING

Yellow, green, black, brown,
  Colours, mix, abound,
Back, forth, up, down,
  Canvas, master, frown.
    (A.G., Cranbrook School, Sydney, Australia.)

STEEPLECHASE

Talk, bed, stirred, slumbers,
  Wake, eat, ache,
Prunes, change, nerves, numbers,
  Start, sprint, gate.

Fence, climb, mud, swarm,
  Hills, dales, fast,
Water, ice, smell, farm,
  Square, finish, last.
        (R.H., Repton, England.)

SYLLABLE POEM

MARTIANS

raid
of the
green Martians
in   flabbable
multi-coloured   ships
wobble   over
and they burst
in pink
blobs
(P.T., Lower Canada College,
Montreal, Canada.)

ANEMONE

The
twisting
dance of the
A n e m o n e
marvel   of   beauty
but stop to think
those arms are
made to
kill
(S.M., Cranbrook School,
Sydney, Australia.)

DESERT

Hot
Lifeless
Unearthly
Ever - stretching
V e g e t a t i o n l e s s
Ever - silent
Motionless
Wasteful
Sand
(D.P., Wilderness School,
Adelaide, Australia.)

BUBBLES

fat
p u f f y
round and long
through the air like
jellyfish   they   roll
and journey through
the   soft   air
till they
drop
(S.B., Rugby, England.)

HAIKU

SMALL TALK

Ossified clichés
Casual superlatives
All bland vocal tics.

(T.R., Lower Canada College,
Montreal, Canada.)

TRAM

Large green ugly bulk,
Rumbling to a noisy stop,
Crashes on its way.

(P.T., The Hill School,
San Francisco, U.S.A.)

DRAGSTER

Will you win this race,
You roaring, smoking dragster?
How fast *can* you go?

(G.S., Scotch College, Launceston,
Australia.)

SPIDER WEB

A thread of silver,
A spider web so fragile,
Glistens in the sun.

(A.H., Repton, England.)

GUINEA PIGS

Guinea pigs are fat
Always eating, never full
Greedy little things.

(R.G., School 52, Moscow,
U.S.S.R.)

PUDDLE

A muddy puddle,
Lying alone in the dirt
Soaking on the ground.

(T.R., Verdun High School,
Montreal, Canada.)

RACING CAR

Racing car so big,
And black, why do *they* win
when
You are on the track?

(D.P., Lyndon Institute,
Vermont, U.S.A.)

MY HAND

My hand is so small,
Sometimes it's tired and dirty,
But it serves me well.

(B.M., St. Peter's College, Adelaide,
Australia.)

CLIMBING TIMBERTOP

Spirit is fading,
The sweat bears heavy on us,
Where is the summit?

(A.B., Geelong Grammar (Timbertop) School, Australia.)

BLACKBOARD

Black and so gruesome,
Glaring out at every class,
Not breaking its stare.

(A.D., Barker College, Sydney,
Australia.)

LAZY CHAIR

Lazily he stands,
Waiting for his heavy guest,
I'm sorry for him.
(G.H., Charles St. School,
Launceston, Australia.)

WAGTAIL

Perching on the fence,
The cheeky willy wagtail,
Struggling for a grip.
(P.V., St. George's School,
Vancouver, Canada.)

FREEDOM

The birds are flying,
Through the spacious, icy air,
Carefree as the wind.
(G.M., The Grange School,
Santiago, Chile.)

TV SET

With blank face it stares,
Its metallic heart so still,
Waiting to be tuned.
(C.R., Friends' School, Hobart,
Australia.)

WITCHETTY GRUB

Small witchetty grub,
Sleeping in a rotting log,
Out of sight in there.
(V.W., Friends' School, Hobart,
Australia.)

MY EYE

I ripped a boy's tie;
He didn't seem too happy;
I've got a black eye.
(G.J., Horace Mann School,
New York, U.S.A.)

THE WINDOW

Captured buzzing fly,
Escape from your clear prison,
Be free forever.
(G.H., The Dragon School,
Oxford, England.)

BUTTERFLY

Settling softly down,
Brilliant colours red and blue—
Stately butterfly.
(P.V., Lower Canada College,
Montreal, Canada.)

FIRE (a multiple haiku)

Tiny little spark,
Just a minute phase of flame,
Concentrated life.

Elixir of death,
Chance may bring it to some
fuel,
Causing birth of flame.

That will grow with time,
Mature, father other tongues,
Of radiant heat.

These also mature,
Reproducing more and more,
Enveloping fuel.

Fire has reached its prime,
The apex of existence,
Symbolized by flame.

This—the time of strength,
Time of greatest heat and light,
Starts to dwindle now.

The brilliant yellow,
And the violent glaring red
Of its youth now fade.

Flame becomes a glow,
The reflection of its height,
This soon fades away.

Sudden gust of wind,
May end this life of beauty,
At each point of life.

Such is life of man,
Is born, grows up, manhood
   gains,
Fades away to death.

God is like this flame,
We sense his heat, see his light,
Yet we grasp Him not.

(K.M., Geelong Grammar School,
                    Australia.)

COMPLETED IMAGE VARIATION

THE ROAD WORKER

He stood there, brawny arms gleaming;
Beads of sweat streamed off his forehead;
His giant frame rose and fell;
He swung his massive dust-caked pick.

(E.M., The King's School, Sydney, Australia.)

RACING CAR

Chrome and steel flashes by on blurred discs;
Exhausts crackle as they expel their smoke;
Acrid rubber is flayed on the hairpin bend;
Man exercises his lust for speed.

(E.B., Lower Canada College, Montreal, Canada.)

WINTER

Water gushes in gutters and down drain-pipes;
Trees creak with wind and rushing gusts;
Inside is warmth and the redness of fires;
We sit and think of summer days gone by.

(S.S., The Grange School, Santiago, Chile.)

CLASSROOM

The desks stretch in broken lines;
A thoughtful hush descends like a curtain;
The wood, carved by generations, runs under my fingers;
I sit waiting for inspiration to come.

(R.L., Repton, England.)

CORROBOREE

The didgeridoo booms over darkened plains;
The light of the fires plays on twisting figures;
They smell of grease, and ochre, and grass;
They seem to writhe on the still-hot earth.

(M.H., Gloucester High School, Australia.)

PIG

The pig is a small, dirty animal;
It goes its way with a series of grunts;
Its smell is close to that of stagnant water;
Still, its piglets are warm and friendly.

(P.L., St. John's School, Winnipeg, Canada.)

FOREMAN

Heavy diesel fumes invade the air;
Men sweat all day from rise to set, for what?
The foreman shouts and raves;
His master is a time schedule.

(A.P., Belmont Hill School, Boston, U.S.A.)

KANGAROO

The bushes stir as if in panic;
The kangaroo bounds head-long down the valley;
Terror has deformed his native grace;
I realize how cruel man must be.

(B.W., Geelong Grammar (Timbertop) School, Australia.)

FORMAL PATTERN

MY BIKE AND I

Zooming down the road I went,
I pranged into a tree;
My bike was twisted, scratched, and bent,
But guess what happened to me?

(R.S., Lower Canada College, Montreal, Canada.)

WHITE INSECT

Small white insect flying past
  Why will you not stop?
Come! Sit on my finger gentle insect;
  I will do you no harm.

Small white insect with feelers thin,
  Delicate wings and tiny legs—
Come! I will do you no harm.

Small white insect, please come to me;
  Why do you have to fly away?
I will do you no harm.

(J.B., Melbourne Grammar School, Melbourne,
Australia.)

ELEGY ON A GREY HARBOUR

The grimy Sydney ferry bravely ploughs,
Lonely across the dish wash harbour grey,
A vicious wind is tipping at her bows,
A plucky craft indeed on such a day.
And as she churns her way through rip and tide,
The motors down below roar on non-stop,
The passengers are huddled up inside,
The captain's calmly steering up on top.
The biting wind sprays salt upon her deck,
The iron rails rust as the wind roars past,
But none of this decay has much effect,
For this stout craft was truly built to last.
Lonely across the dish wash harbour grey,
A plucky craft indeed on such a day.

(M.A., Cranbrook School, Sydney, Australia.)

OPTIC PATTERNS

THE WINDOW

```
The      window
m e a s u r e s
e v e r y t h i n g
I          s e e
a  man  with
o u t   f e e t
small  children
without  bodies
what  will  not  fit
is  incomplete  forever
```
(P.T., Lower Canada College,
Montreal, Canada.)

THE BULL
MENACING   DEADLY
D U M B
P O W E R F U L
R U M B L I N G
C H A R G E
C A P E

OLÉ
OLÉ   OLÉ
POWER   STRENGTH
CAPE RED ANGER
SWORD

T   DEATH   T
H   H
U   U
N   N
D   D
E   E
R   R
I   I
N   N
G   G

(C.S., Cranbrook School, Sydney,
Australia.)

Jellyfish

Jelly-like
folding, spreading
oozing, melting, colourless
stinging, paralysing, eating
Innardless, boneless, brainless

```
T        W        B        R        S             H
E        A        E        E        E             U
N        V        N        A        A             N
T        I        D        C        R             G
A        N        I        H        C             R
C        G        N        I        H             Y
L                 G        N        I
E        W                 G        N             K
S        E                          G             I
         A        S                               L
F        V        T        O        S             L
L        I        R        U        W             E
O        N        E        T        I             R
   O     G        T        W        N
      W           C        A        G
         I        H        R        I
            N     I        D        N
               G     N     S        G
                        G
```

(A.K., Cranbrook School, Sydney, Australia)

Siamese Cat

Boisterous monkey
black - faced
black - eared

elegant
long
tailed
yet
how

mischievous
playful, daring
yet how faithfully
canine, more like
a puppy with its need for adoration

(R.M., Repton, England)

GENERAL

THE CAT

Prowling, growling, searching, scrounging
For the tasty morsel;
Slowly slithering, slinking, slissing
Like an electric coil.
Eyes with an emerald glow,
Fixed like radar on the prey.
Tail twitching like a metronome
Slowly slithering, slinking, slissing
Bounce . . . pounce.

(G.S., Geelong Grammar School, Australia.)

THE NOOSE

It waits there;
   The footsteps echo,
and the gaol is quiet.

It hangs there;
   The footsteps continue,
and the world is quiet.

It beckons there;
   The footsteps stop,
and the man is quiet.

It swings there;
   The feet dangle,
and the man is dead.

(P.G., Lower Canada College,
Montreal, Canada.)

FROST

The hand reaches out—
   Cold, clammy, blue.
The eyes are fixed;
They see no longer.

(P.V., Repton, England.)

CAGES

Birds,
Trapped birds,
In cages,
Crying aloud to be set free to fly,
            to jump, to sing.
Birds,
Sad birds,
In cages,
As darkness comes their tails droop low,
Their heads fall,
They are mere shadows of
The singing birds outside.

            (G.V., The Grange School, Santiago, Chile.)

COIN MACHINE

A quarter in, and pull the knob,
Clackety-crash, clackety-crash.
Pull the lever, hope it doesn't stick,
Clackety, clackety, clackety, click.
Whirring motor, flashing disc,
Tension, tension, clackety-click,
Spewing coins, it's money-sick,
Tumble, tumble, clackety-click.

            (A.L., Lyndon Institute, Vermont, U.S.A.)

THE POWER SHOVEL

With a roar and a cloud of smoke,
The sleeping monster wakes;
Amid metallic groans,
With mechanical constipation,
It lumbers noisily forward,
Sinking its hungry steel teeth,
Into the defenceless soil.

            (I.M., Merchant Taylors' School, England.)

POETRY

They asked a true poet
(Who *said* that he was true)
To write of warmth and wonder,
Faith and laughter,
But the poet only wrote.

(A.L., Geelong Grammar School, Australia.)

POETRY

A fleeting glimpse
Of a new world
Exciting, mysterious.
Where the mind can romp freely
And discover new ways
Of carrying dreams.

Roadway through
A thousand thoughts,
Gateway to a thousand images
Each one living, breathing
Infused with life—
Flowing from the pen
So one can feel the wind,
See far landscapes.

(C.L., Cranbrook School, Sydney, Australia.)

SELECT BIBLIOGRAPHY

1. APPLEGATE, M.: *Helping Children Write*—Evanston, Ill.: Row, Peterson and Co., 1961.

2. BALDWIN, M.: *Poetry Without Tears*—London: Routledge and Kegan Paul, 1959.

3. BROOKS, C., and WARREN, R. P.: *Understanding Poetry* (3rd Edition)—New York: Holt, Rinehart and Winston Inc., 1960.

4. CLEGG, A. B. (ed.): *The Excitement of Writing*—London: Chatto and Windus (Educ.) Ltd., 1964.

5. COOPER, G., and HOURD, M.: *Coming into their Own*—London: Heinemann Ltd., 1959.

6. CROSS, K. G. W., and MARSH, D. R. C.: *Poetry Reading and Understanding*—Melbourne: F. W. Cheshire, 1966.

7. DRUCE, Robert: *The Eye of Innocence*—Leicester: Brockhampton Press Ltd., 1965.

8. FORD, Boris (ed.): *Young Writers, Young Readers*—London: Hutchinson of London, 1960.

9. HOLBROOK, David: *English for Maturity*—London: Cambridge University Press, 1961.

10. HOOK, J. N.: *Writing Creatively*—Boston: D. C. Heath and Co., 1963.

11. KNAPP, Edgar: *Introduction to Poetry*—Wichita, Ka.: McCormick Mathers Publishing Co. Inc., 1965.

12. LANGDON, Margaret: *Let the Children Write Poetry*—London: Longman's and Co., 1961.

13. LEWIS, C. Day: *Poetry for You*—Oxford: Basil Blackwell, 1959.

14. MEARNS, H.: *Creative Power*—New York: Dover Publications Inc., 1958.

15. MOSBY, F., and THOMAS, J. K.: *Sense, Feeling, and Thought*—London: Oxford University Press, 1946.

16. O'DONNELL, M. J.: *Feet On the Ground*—London: Blackie and Son Ltd., 1946.

17. REEVES, James: *Understanding Poetry*—London: Heinemann Educational Books Ltd., 1965.

18. ROWE, A. W., and EMMENS, P.: *English Through Experience* —London: Blond Educational Ltd., 1963.

19. SWEETKIND, Morris: *Teaching Poetry in the High School*— New York: The Macmillan Company, 1964.

20. WALTER, Nina: *Let Them Write Poetry*—New York: Holt, Rinehart and Winston Inc., 1962.

INDEX